T0103893

BEING USED OF
GOD

A Reed Shaken in the Wind

DINO B. NICHOLAS

WestBow
PRESS
A DIVISION OF THOMAS NELSON

Copyright © 2013 Dino B. Nicholas.

All rights reserved. No part of this book may be used or reproduced by
any means, graphic, electronic, or mechanical, including photocopying,
recording, taping or by any information storage retrieval system
without the written permission of the publisher except in the case
of brief quotations embodied in critical articles and reviews.

Unless otherwise indicated, all Scripture quotations in this
publication are from the Holy Bible King James Version
©1976 Thomas Nelson, INC. Nashville Tennessee.

Scripture taken from the King James Version of the Bible.

Scripture quotations taken from the New American Standard Bible®,
Copyright © 1960, 1962, 1963, 1968, 1971, 1972, 1973, 1975, 1977, 1995 by
The Lockman Foundation. Used by permission." (www.Lockman.org)

WestBow Press books may be ordered through booksellers or by contacting:

WestBow Press
A Division of Thomas Nelson
1663 Liberty Drive
Bloomington, IN 47403
www.westbowpress.com
1 (866) 928-1240

Because of the dynamic nature of the Internet, any web addresses or
links contained in this book may have changed since publication and
may no longer be valid. The views expressed in this work are solely those
of the author and do not necessarily reflect the views of the publisher,
and the publisher hereby disclaims any responsibility for them.

Any people depicted in stock imagery provided by Thinkstock are
models, and such images are being used for illustrative purposes only.
Certain stock imagery © Thinkstock.

ISBN: 978-1-4908-1695-1 (sc)

Library of Congress Control Number: 2013921404

Printed in the United States of America.

WestBow Press rev. date: 12/05/2013

CONTENTS

DEDICATION

I lovingly and tenderly dedicate this book to the person who inspired it. With her life and spirit she has shown me what it truly means to be Used of God. Self-less, God-fearing and courageous she has along with the Holy Spirit propelled me into my God given purpose.

From my vantage point of being her husband, I have watched her grow in her relationship with God, I have seen her influence expand beyond borders – she is an end time saint. Her name is Lorri-Ann, my companion, our children's champion and mentor.

Thank you so very much for being here, you are the best Christian I know.

Darling, Pumpkin I love you.

How can one soul make such a difference!

ACKNOWLEDGEMENTS

I want to thank Pastors Kirk and Natasha Campbell for their inspiration and support on this project, your help was invaluable. Thanks to Ms. Althea Smikle who helped to edit this work, I could not have done it without you. To my family who has endured my ups and downs, your support has been the corner stone of my life. To my Powerhouse family thanks for putting up with me as your pastor for six years, the word I now write was birthed in that season. To my Bishop, your life has inspired me to be used of God. Maranatha your cheers are always in my ears thanks for your support. To my family at Lighthouse Family Worship Center a great thank you.

FOREWORD 1

This is a message penned by a man of God – echoing the heart of God. Being used of God is the ultimate plan of God for every believer. This speaks of the divine purpose enfolded in the life of a believer and one's prophetic destiny as one begins to walk the path of faith.

Any man who has been graced by God as one "being used of God" to inspire faith and to activate people to trust with all their hearts and to passionately pursue him in complete obedience to his word, is to be highly commended. For these are the teachers and mentors that are so sadly lacking in the world today and are so desperately needed.

It's all well and good we talk about what we are doing for God or dream of all the great things we want to accomplish in His name. But it is quite a different thing to put yourself in the position to be used of God. What we have in these times is a lot of talk, theatrics but no substance, no strength of character, no life. This has become a means to an end for many a way to fame and fortune, even big time business, a way to earn the almighty dollar.

Being used of God would suggest someone who is a "living testament", an epistle of one whose life can be seen and read by all men. Someone who has logged on to God, in total surrender and is now dedicated to a life of obedience to God. The Bible calls such a person an epistle.

The opposite of an "epistle" would be a false teacher, a counterfeit, a look alike, or a wolf in sheep's clothing. It takes someone who is "tender and pliable" in the hands of God, someone who has been honed by the Masters hands, someone who is like a reed shaking in the wind. This is a prophetic expression of saint totally at the mercy of God, to speak the truth. You must first live it before you can point someone in that path. You must first do it before you qualify to tell it.

Bishop Robert McIntosh
Founder & President
Maranatha Ministries International
Jamaica

FOREWORD 2

We grow up in Christendom being encouraged to offer ourselves to be 'used of God'. We sing songs proclaiming that our greatest desire is to be used by God. It sounds holy and feels like the right thing to say. Then God calls our bluff.

Dino Nicholas has put so eloquently into words what I am finding out in my quest to be pleasing to God yet relevant in this life. I only wish that he had done this sooner so I would not have felt 'blindsided' when the rigors of the process hit me! The pretty words belie the challenging procedure… but I am being selfish.

This is a timely presentation of the truth about wanting to do what God wants. In a world where everything is presented as a quick fix and a lovely picture, one man dares to step up and present the 'behind the scenes' version, so that we who are walking this path learn first of all that we are not doing something wrong why our lives are not coming out 'as advertised', but in actuality are being processed aright. Then we find in his expose the encouragement and the support needed to 'hold strain' and keep on going.

A Jamaican proverb says: "he who feels it, knows it!" I have seen Dino evolve over the last twenty years from a zealous teenager, ready to take over the world into a fearless Prophet and Preacher, established in the Word of God. He has been tested, shaken, tried and proven through the trials of life. He has faced traumas that have destroyed lesser men and has remained standing. As Pastor, he has stood, not just for himself, but for so many of us who lean on him for counsel, encouragement, advice and comfort - and he is still here!

Now he has found a voice for the discoveries he has made in his experiences. The things he has taught and used to encourage many, have now found expression through a media that will touch many more lives and encourage them to keep on going until they ultimately realize that they ARE being used of God. May the Lord bless Dino Nicholas' faithfulness.

Patricia Ramsey
International Psalmist
Massachusetts

INTRODUCTION

Matt.11:7 "And as they departed, Jesus began to say unto the multitude concerning, John, What went ye out into the wilderness to see? A reed shaken with the wind?"

Jesus' describes, John as one of the tenderest plants, a reed, but not only a reed but a reed flourishing outside of its usual environment. What went you out into the wilderness to see? Not a reed, maybe some other spectacle, but not the most tender of plants.

However, God chose to set a reed in the wilderness. God's methodology in using his servants is striking at best, as his ways far supersede our thoughts. To be used of God sounds glorious, it might even conjure up thoughts of spotlights, great wealth, riches and much fame. To be used of God sounds so good. Your parents might be proud; friends and well wishers will be in abundance… to be known to be used of God.

As our contemporary history has shown us, to be used of God seems to bring to those most fortunate instant fame, television contracts and great wealth. We have seen the very successful tele-evangelists in their sparkling suits, well gelled hair. Healing the sick, not even the most powerful president in the world can heal the sick in Jesus name, only someone who has been used of God, or so we are led to believe. Our modern day examples for the most part betray the high ideal that God places on a vessel that is being used by God.

As I study the scriptures and come into greater alignment to God and his purpose, a deep conflict gathers intensity within me as I desire to be used by God however I desire to be treated as the world has dictated to me. For example I have some inalienable rights, freedom, happiness and basic necessities that a man of any status must attain. Such as, to own at least one home, drive an automobile and be in a position to buy anything he wants within good reason. All these are great and I believe God wants us happy and free, our families to have a safe and secure financial and physical future. And with all that is said, there is this conflict within me over one question, "Am I willing to pay whatever it costs, to be used of God?"

Many of my pastor friends tell me, I don't have to give it all up, use wisdom. But then another question comes "Does the clay have any say in the hand of the master?" Does the clay jar have a say in how he is made... no! Hence he has no say in how he is being used.

To be used of God, what does this mean? Is this important? What are the qualifications? And who does God use? Are there any examples of persons being used of God today, can we draw inspiration from their lives and from the lives of the men and women of the scriptures who were used of God.

We are called servants of God. We don't hear that much nowadays, as this is not a popular term, it connotes lowliness, abasement and it doesn't fit into the modern teaching that we are all leaders, but there is no higher calling in God than that of a servant. Why is this so maligned in the Church? Jesus teaches us that if we want to be the greatest we must be the servant of all. As we explore the topic, I pray the presence of the Holy Ghost, the one who serves will envelope us and bring us into a greater knowledge of what it really means to be used of God.

A REED SHAKEN
IN THE WIND

The ministry of John the Baptist has all the marks of an earthly vessel being effectively used of God. His birth and his ministry speak of God's sovereignty over the affairs of men. As we study this topic of being Used of God, it is important to understand two things.

- What it means to be used of God from God's perspective?
- What should be the response of the vessel being chosen and the process that these vessels or lives go through in reaching the highest of calls, to be a servant of God.

Much of what we call Christian service today is a far cry from what Christ intended it to be. Christian service, in a lot of cases, at the highest level is just a matriculation process from the best seminaries or Bible schools of students who mostly have started out with a desire to serve. However, as many have found out as they get involved in the system, service turns into being served. They get caught up in the glamour and power of Christianity and their true purpose is eroded.

The decades of the eighties and nineties, taught us some very powerful lessons that we will take time to heed today. Many mega- churches were successfully launched. The Church moved from out of the shadows of the western culture becoming a force in many societies, based on sheer numbers. The television airwaves were littered with numerous televangelists. Dynasties and empires were formed as the mega-ministries grew, thirty thousand and more in membership. For a while this seemed like a good thing as it appeared the gospel was increasing and the end of the age was imminent.

Christianity became a place for stars. Only the brightest and most eloquent were given the spotlight, those who seemed to always have a word that would appease the masses. Only those were sought after. Many of them had high price tags but they were still able to pull the crowd. The messages reflected their star like status, as prosperity became the message of the moment. The blessing of God was our Christian mantra. Our Christian greeting was "God is good all the time all the time God is good." What we were really saying is life is good all the time and all the time life is good. The Church was enjoying the good times, land prices were inexpensive so many expanded beyond their need, and in an attempt to keep up with the Jones many conferences were launched to outdo other mega-conferences. The question was who could attract the best speakers; we were all over ourselves with success.

Out of this phenomenon was spawned the seeker sensitive Christian, which led to the seeker sensitive church, seeker sensitive church programmes, books, comics and movies. Several best-selling books were written, many mega-conferences were held as we celebrated our success and good fortune. Then it all started to crumble, several of our leading lights were pulled down from their lofty heights through sin or illicit behaviors. Mega –ministries were deserted, rubble and ruin reigned where there once were glorious edifices and the enemies of God had much to say against God.

The Church developed a culture of professional leaders, everybody was a leader, and we were encouraged to rise to the zenith of our potential. Nothing is wrong with that we need to strive to be the best we can be, however, when self actualization becomes our highest ideal and not self denial as taught by Christ, we are headed for ruin. In our mad haste to become better; better people, better leaders, we brought in the hype of self improvement. Seminar after seminar was created to bring out the best that was in us. Serving Christ and making him known was no longer the goal, it was Christ wants us all better. That is, he died for us to have the best life we could possibly carve out for ourselves. That is if we followed the seven steps to fulfill your heavenly potential, now for your best gift you could have the whole series plus a bonus. The Gospel of Jesus Christ was reduced to 'your best gift'. I wonder what would happen to the widow and her mite in this generation.

The Messianic message is being pushed to the back of the bus. What message? Jesus said this "I did not come to be served but to serve" (Matt.20:28). The importance of this message cannot be understated, as he was not just saying that he came to serve others, a doctrine that some have taken to the other extreme. In fact he was saying that he came to serve God. It was the Father's plan and he agreed with it and submitted himself to the process because he loved the Father. This mind needs to be drastically restored in the Church:-

> "Let this mind be in you, which was also in Christ Jesus: who being in the form of God thought it not robbery to be equal to God: But made Himself of no reputation and took upon himself the form of a servant and was made in the likeness of men:" Philippians 2:5-7

Jesus showed that he was a true son by totally submitting his life into his Father's hands. The culmination of this perfect submission was seen and heard on the Cross, when he cried out with his last breath

> "Father into your hand I commend my spirit: and having said this he gave up the ghost." Luke 23:46

To the very end he trusted his Father; we see where the apostles and early church fathers faced death with the same attitude, to serve God to the very end of life, no matter what the end was they were giving praise to God. We recall the death of Stephen:-

> "And they stoned Stephen, calling upon God, and saying Lord Jesus receive my spirit." Acts7:59.

The Apostle Paul declared in the face of imminent death,-

> "For I am now ready to be offered, and the time of my departure is at hand. I have fought a good fight, I have finished my course, and I have kept the faith: Henceforth there is laid up for me a crown of righteousness which the Lord the righteous judge shall give me at that day: and not me only, but unto all them also that love his appearing." 2 Tim. 4:6-8

Jesus was their example and they served to the bitter end not drawing back to save their own lives, it seemed logical to them to die in those fashions because it was their desire to be used of God. The Bible is littered with so many examples of saints who paid the highest price and they did it in the mode of their one leader, Jesus Christ. To serve their Lord was their greatest desire no matter what it meant.

The message of service, being a bond slave of God is now more than ever relevant to the body of Christ as she comes to realize who she is before her Lord. I believe that the Church as it is now cannot be used effectively by the Spirit of God as she is too arrogant and is in a state of backsliding. The Laodicean Church aptly describes our position, Rev. 3:17

> "You say, I am rich, I have everything I want. I do not need a thing! And you don't realize that you are wretched and miserable and poor and blind and naked."

Jesus' observation of the Church was different from the views held by the Church herself. For the Church to turn around we must turn back to Him –Jesus Christ. 1Sam.7:3-4

> And Samuel spoke unto all the house of Israel, saying, "If you do return unto the Lord with all your hearts, then put away strange gods and Ashtoreths from among you, and prepare your hearts unto the Lord, and serve him only: and he will deliver you out of the hands of the Philistines". Then the children of Israel did put away Baalim and Ashtoreths and served the Lord only.

Israel destroyed their idols and worshipped only the Lord. There is a turning to God that is required of his servants, if we are to be used of God we must be totally surrendered to him. If God is going to fully endow us with himself (his Holy Spirit), we must be willing to fully surrender our lives to him. Outside of this there is no way we can be used of God. The highest calling of a saint of God is to be used by a Holy God.

<u>John</u>

The life of John, the one called the baptizer, is of great significance to our study and definition of our topic. Called from before he was conceived and named, he was destined by God to perform a particular task.

> "And many of the children of Israel shall he turn to the Lord their God. And he shall go before him in the spirit and power of Elijah, to turn the hearts of the fathers to the children, and the disobedient to the wisdom of the just; to make ready a people prepared for the Lord" Luke 1:16-17

The importance of John as a vessel of God cannot be overstated as he was blessed to be filled with the Holy Spirit when he was still in his mother's womb (Luke 1:15). Such preparation of this vessel by God needs to be noted by us all. Even though I believe that John was a special individual for a specific time to accomplish a specific task, I strongly believe that God is still preparing his people today maybe in this fashion or maybe another so that they might be used of God.

So important was his task, that the angel Gabriel struck his father Zechariah dumb so that he would not have the opportunity to speak a negative word over the life of his baby. A chosen vessel, carved out by God to be used for God's purpose only.

God, through the holy angel Gabriel, set before Zechariah and us God's purpose for creating his people. Each one of us like John was designed with a purpose in mind, and this purpose was established by our Creator so we could be used of God to fulfill his intended plan. Like clay in the hands of a master potter, we are molded to fit his plans. Thus our existence has meaning. We are not an afterthought, but we were designed for a predetermined destiny. And oddly enough it was all God's plan. Mankind however, in our sinful nature has carved out a social structure for humans to live in and attain. Just like the men who thought they could build a tower and reach heaven, so that their names would last generations, so we today have constructed our own plans; which are in many cases in direct contrast to God's plans for our lives.

To be used of God means: - to be selected, molded and equipped by God to accomplish a set purpose in the earth that He (God) has already established. As we study the life of John we are going to be confronted with the reality that, humanity is wasted outside of knowing and accomplishing the plans of God for it.

Everything in creation was designed by God and is to be used of God to fulfill his eternal purpose. The fish in the sea, the fowl of air, even the smallest ant, and every facet of creation functioning in its divine purpose lends itself to the continuance of God's purpose on the earth. The leaf falls to the ground the ant dices it up for food, the bug eats up what is left of the leaf and its dung fertilizes the soil that makes nutrients for the tree to continue to grow and on it goes. We see the divine order of God in creation, so I must ask, what about man?

The psalmist asks the same question. "What is man, that thou art mindful of him…?" Ps. 8:4-6. So what is it about us that the God of the Universe has chosen to use us, to be mindful of us? The Psalmist writes, "for thou has made him a little lower than the angels and hast crowned him with glory and honor" Ps 8:5 KJV. Man, made a little lower than the angels but crowned or covered with glory and honor, what a great privilege to be chosen by God.

The prophet John points out the significant place given to us by God. Let us get to the meat of the definition. To understand, what it means to be used of God we must understand certain things.

1) God's providence or sovereignty over his creation
2) Understanding God's original intent,
3) Understanding the process that God will take us through to make us ready for his use
4) Understanding the response of the vessel.

A further definition of being used of God is to come under the control of the Holy Spirit as you yield yourself to His (God's) original Plan and pleasure for that moment of your life.

To be effectively used of God three things must come into synchronization, *the right place, the right person and the right time.* These three very important distinctives will be expounded on in a later chapter, but I want you to get familiar with the terms. To be effectively used of God requires us to be in the place that He desires. The Bible declares that we are created for his pleasure (Luke 12:32). The word pleasure as defined by the Oxford Dictionary states: - gratification, fulfillment, delight, a feeling of happy satisfaction and enjoyment. God's intention for us is to be used by him to accomplish his predetermined purpose.

So one question must be on the mind of the child of God, What will give my Lord pleasure - today? To come under the control of the Holy Spirit as we yield ourselves to him takes real determination, especially in a world that is getting more and more anti-Christ. There are so many distractions to occupy the attention of the saints of God. In fact the world is contending for our attention. The world wants to fill our eyes with all of its glamorous images. Everything is clamoring for the attention of our senses. To consistently come under the control of the Holy Spirit will take a conscious and concerted effort on our part, to remain focused. To be called to this type of lifestyle is to court suffering, as we stand the chance of being ridiculed, laughed at, and misunderstood or even just being passed over for seeming to be irrelevant to our generation.

Our sad attempts, as believers in Christ, to consistently fit into the world around us, have made us spiritually impotent and useless to God. How are we supposed to pull down principalities and powers over our cities when we are trusting in their economic models to survive? We have not separated ourselves from the very world we are at war with. There must be a drastic paradigm shift in our thinking for us to be useful to God in this time. Our attendance at services only serve to keep our consciences clear before God, we foolishly comfort ourselves.

We must wean ourselves from the lure of this world because its attractiveness is what kills the plan of God in our lives; in the midst of our studying John's life let us look at one who was mightily used of God, different time, different set of circumstances, but the same timeless principles. A man born in time, seemingly out of his element, not prepared by the world standards but was equipped perfectly by the Lord to be used to deliver an entire nation, let us look at Moses.

Moses – Designed and Designated to be Deliverer

From his birth, Moses was designed by God to accomplish a purpose only He could have designated upon the life of a human. Conceived during the brutal years of Israel's enslavement in Egypt, Moses was God's answer to the cry of his people to be delivered from their lives of imprisonment and oppression. The Bible declares this of the baby Moses:-

> "And the woman conceived and bore a son: and when she saw him that he was a goodly child, she hid him three months." Exodus 2:2

By reason of a mother's love for her child she decided to protect Moses from the edict of the Pharaoh, that all male children born at that time must be put to death. The Bible said that she saw that he was a goodly child, a mother's determined care or God's providence, one cannot tell. However, the mother's action kept Moses alive and furthermore her plans positioned Moses for his future use by God.

> "And when she could no longer hide him, she took for him an ark of bulrushes, and daubed it with slime and pitch, and put the child therein; and she laid it in the flags by the river bank. And his sister stood afar off, to wit what would be done to him.

And the daughter of Pharaoh came down to wash herself at the river; and her maidens walked along by the riverside, and when she saw the ark among the flags she sent her maid to fetch it." Exodus 2:3-5

Sheer coincidence or design orchestrated by a living God. I rather choose the latter. The odds are too great that this was an arbitrary act. His mother's desperate actions, led her to make an ark put her son in it and let it float down the river, why? Verse 4 gives her highly reasoned position on the matter. She set her young daughter afar off to watch and to know what would be done to him. In other words she put the life of Joseph in God's hands. She had protected him as far a she could; now it was God's turn.

What was her point of reference for this act? There was no such behavior prerecorded. Could it be that only after we let go can God step in and do wondrously. What were the chances that the daughter of Pharaoh would come along the river at that point? Even if it was her regular routine and Moses' Mom studied her for weeks and set up her acts to collide with the Pharaohs daughter's bath time, so many things could have gone wrong – but God. He is the great designer of life's outcomes, that if we only trust him even when we can't perceive him, we will see the glorious works of God. Desperation plus a desire for good hygiene was God's salvation design for his chosen vessel to deliver his people from slavery.

It gets better, the daughter of Pharaoh took him in at that moment, and Moses' sister ran up to her obviously with a preplanned story; "shall I go and call to thee a nurse of the Hebrew women, that she may nurse the child for thee." Exodus 2:7

Without thinking, maybe she was unable to have a child of her own, we were never told, but God used her in her current state to protect his plan.

> "And Pharaoh's daughter said to her, go. And the maid went and called the child's mother. And Pharaoh's daughter said unto her, take this child away and nurse it for me, and I will give thee thy wages. And the woman took the child and nursed it." Exodus2:8-9

What a master stroke of genius, this could only have been designed by God. Moses mother was now being paid to nurse and grow up her own child under the protection of the state, that same state that had issued an edict for his execution.

Born a slave, but he grew as a prince of Egypt in the home of Pharaoh why? What purpose could this serve? Being born a slave and living as a slave would not have prepared him to be an effective deliverer of God's people. He would have been an effective rebel leader with his own agenda, as we saw later in his life when he took matters into his own hands and killed an Egyptian to deliver his brethren from being beaten. God was not preparing an Egyptian killer, but rather a man who would take down an entire nation and all their gods.

Many times we sabotage God's plan for our lives, when we learn of his plans but are unprepared to do it his way. Though Moses was called of God, he was not yet qualified to be a deliverer. Why? He lacked the fear and the awareness of God. Too many of us leaders jump into action like Moses, totally unaware of God's larger plan for our lives. We don't need to learn more leadership principles to lead God's people; we need to know the fear of God which is the beginning of wisdom. God had to empty Moses of the world's wisdom before he could use him. Forty years later when God finally turned up, Moses was a broken man, devoid of all self confidence. He was drawn to God by a burning bush, an ordinary occurrence in the Sinai desert; dry bushes caught fire frequently because of the heat. However, he had become so aware of God through forty years of processing that a seemingly ordinary bush fire could draw his attention. God used an everyday incident to manifest his presence as Moses was now able to see what others could not perceive. God uses the ordinary things of life to reveal himself to those who are drawn to him by His Spirit. When God finally after many generations spoke to a man, his man, his response would have seemed pathetic in the world's view, but it was apostolic and heavenly from God's perspective. Moses said;

> "Who am I that I should go unto Pharaoh, and that I should bring forth the children of Israel out of Egypt." Exodus 3:11

The world seems to build a man up to destroy him, but God pulls a man down so that he can build him up. Your qualifications do not impress God; Moses was the most qualified man at forty to lead God's people out and God chased him into the wilderness to be pressed and reformed for the next forty years before he could use him. Are we willing to pay the price that is required to be used of God?

At the age of eighty when we rediscover the former prince of Egypt, he was keeping the flock of Jethro forty years watching sheep was God's plan, His university training, his designer program to build the best leader to deliver his children out of over four hundred years of slavery. I guarantee you that this would not have been the world's plan, nor dare I say the plan of the Church. We would have jumped for Moses at forty in the prime of his life to do the work. The Bible teaches us not to look at the outward appearance but to focus on the inner man. We judge too quickly by natural manifestations. God wants to use us to accomplish his divine plan for our lives, but we must develop the patience and the fear of God before we can be effectively used of God.

Moses' parents are not mentioned, only their tribe, Levi which means praise; however John's parents were named, they came from the same tribe. They were not under Egyptian type slavery but they were under Roman law and taxation, slavery without the whips, but with the same weapon, fear. Hence, it was in a similar context that John was born, to be used of God, not as a deliverer of his people but as the forerunner of the deliverer. The actions of his parents are of great significance as were those of Moses' parents. **I challenge any parent reading this book to consider your actions in light of what is being revealed to you by the Holy Spirit, and bring yourself to the place where you determine in your heart to align you child's full destiny to God's plans and not what society dictates or even what you desire through your shortsighted vision of your offspring.**

We see, in the life of John, where God took special care in preparing John's parents.

> "And they had no child, that Elizabeth was barren, and they both *were* well stricken in years."

Just like Abraham and Sarah generations before, where God allowed barrenness to precede the blessing. God used the period of barrenness to prepare the parents of the chosen seed to be processed and prepared so that they would be in alignment with God's will for that seed. How many of us have been driven away from the true calling in our lives because we had parents who were unconcerned about the will of God for their child's life. Abraham and Sarah desperately followed God; they were willing to obey His every word after the miracle of the birth of their first son. Abraham was willing to take his son Isaac up to Mount Mariah and offer him up to God as a sacrifice, just because God told him to. For thirty years the Father of the faith of Israel followed God in a strange land, whilst he waited on the promised seed. So full of God was he that his desire for Isaac was no different from God's desire for Isaac.

Good parents will always do the best for their children, giving them the right tools to succeed in life. However if those parents are not aligned to the plan of God for their lives, they will also cause the purpose of God to be derailed in their children. "Success" might follow, but true success is to do the will of the Lord. Jesus said in John 4:34,

> "My meat is to do the will of him that sent me and to finish his work."

God's purpose must be foremost in our lives because, if it is not we will be incapable of imparting it into the lives of others, especially our children. What might seem good to us may not be the plan of God for their lives. I recall a testimony I heard of a young woman who became a lawyer because her father said so, he was a lawyer, her brothers were lawyers and so it was natural for her to join the law firm, natural for everyone except her. So for many years she obeyed the wishes of her father and family and became a highly successful lawyer. All the time her dream was to become a violinist. She loved music with all her heart but was never given a chance to prepare or practice as it was seen as a distraction. It was at the age of 42 years after the death of her father she found the courage to follow what her true calling was. Can you imagine if she was allowed to follow her passions from a youth, maybe at 42 years she would be living her dream of playing in the Philharmonic Orchestra rather than just starting? So many years were lost.

A Reed shaken in the Wind

Zacharias and Elizabeth understood that this child was chosen of God, and so they took special care in his upbringing. Luke 1:80 –

> "And the child grew and waxed strong in spirit, and was in the desert till the day of his showing unto Israel."

There is something about the desert that God seems to love as almost all his chosen vessels had a desert or wilderness experience before the commencement of their ministry before God. We just read about Moses' desert experience, King David lived in a cave for some time, Elijah, Abraham, Jacob all had some time in the desert and the list does not end here. There is something about this place that the world never chooses as the place of preparation, and in John's case presentation.

The desert speaks of dryness, harsh living conditions, and loneliness. It is hard to come up with a positive line of thinking as we describe the desert. However, the desert is ideally suited to the putting away of the flesh and the strengthening of the spirit man. Jesus was in the desert for forty days before he was launched into public ministry. It appears that this is the place of greatest confrontation with the enemies of our souls. To have come into public ministry without first overcoming the enemy in the secluded place of the desert, where no one will ever see your greatest triumph or take part in your encounter like Moses, is not recommended. So when you tell your story there will be some in the audience who will shudder in disbelief, shaking their heads signaling that what you are saying cannot be true. But this is the place of your most important and intimate moments with God. What would convince parents to send their only child into the wilderness? Only God could convince them. "He grew and waxed strong in spirit." This is the result of completing your desert course, strong in spirit. It is said of Jesus in Luke 4:14:-

> "Then Jesus went back full of and under the power of the Holy Spirit into Galilee, and the fame of Him spread through the whole region round about."

Upon leaving the desert Jesus was full of the power of the Holy Spirit. Moses when he left the Sinai to return to Egypt, he was full of the power of God and so will we be today if we allow the Holy Spirit to lead us into our wilderness experience.:-

"And Jesus being full of the Holy Spirit returned from the Jordan and was led by the spirit into the wilderness." Luke 4:1

It was the Holy Spirit that led him; he did not just wander into the wilderness, he was not sent to the wilderness as punishment. He was gracefully sent there. Oh, how God wants to lead us there. Our greatest victory awaits us; our most intimate moments with God loom, just over there in the wilderness. This leading might come in the form of losing a job, a broken marriage, a great disappointment, the loss of someone or something dear to you. Whatever it is let the Holy Spirit lead you there, that's where you will see the burning bush that never burns up. That's where you will put your staff down and it turns into a snake, that's where you see heaven's gateway as Jacob saw it at Bethel. The spirit of religion has robbed us of our most tender moments in God. The past decades have been filled with teachings that have discredited the dry places as satanic, claiming that God only wants us blessed and highly favored; every bad thing is from the devil because God is good all the time. This is so far from the reality of God; yes he is good all the time, but he will take his choice vessels through some trying moments to reveal his precious truth. The blasting of amplifiers and electrical instruments, the razzle dazzle of the modern day preacher has done much to lead us away from the place of encounter.

We are still looking for Jesus in the palace when he came in a stable; we build beautiful church edifices and cry and bawl every Sunday for God to thunder. We have become as loud and as boisterous as the four hundred and forty prophets of Baal who were crying out for a visitation. None came then and none will be coming now. It took a man who had been with God, come from a desert place, was broken in spirit and contrite in heart, only he would God answer. Only he would God use to bring fire. So it was then so it must be now. God is asking us today:-

Are you willing to develop the <u>passion</u> that will <u>produce</u> the <u>power</u> that will bring eternal change?

If your answer is yes, then the wilderness is a necessary stop on the way to empowerment.

<u>A Spectacle... God's End Time Servant</u>

> "What went ye out into the wilderness to see? A reed shaken in the wind?" Matt 11:7b

A reed is defined to be a water marsh plant with a tall hollow stem, suited for wet places. By its design it would appear that the reed grass or plant was created to exist in swamp like conditions. I am no botanist, but what is clear to me is that plants will thrive or grow best in the environment suited for them. There are some plants that grow only in the tropics; others only grow where it's cold and wintry.

Naturally speaking, a plant cannot be transplanted into conditions hostile to it and survive. You should not plant orchids in the North Pole; similarly you would not plant a water lily in the Sahara desert. Yet God decided to put his precious reed, called John, in the wilderness.

The clay pot has no say in how it is being made, or for what purpose, the potter decides its use. So too our Lord, he decides our use. John was a spectacle – used of God to call God's people to repentance and to prepare the way of the Lord. The Bible teaches:-

> Ananias and Caiaphas being the high priests
> the word of God came unto John the son of
> Zacharias in the wilderness." Luke 3:2

Positioned by God in the wilderness so that he could hear God's voice away from the noise and clamor of the town, this reed did not only survive but thrived in the wilderness. God's way might not seem to make sense to us but we must learn to trust him. We are called to thrive in places where others think we cannot survive.

The Apostle Paul declared "We live and move and have our being in Christ." (Acts 17:28). There is a dependence on the Lord that modern day technology is stripping away from us. Now hear me well, I am not anti-technology I believe it is good in most cases, however, our quick dependence on them rather than God has led us away from developing a strong relationship with the Lord, to just a superficial Sunday morning religious experience. An experience lacking any type reality of God or his word, in many cases doctors can help us where once prayer was the only answer, but let me ask who is praying for the doctors. Prayer is always the answer; it can never be replaced by successful medications or surgical procedures. We are vessels in the master's hands and we must learn to trust God like the saints of old.

Not much information is given about John's living conditions in the Word, however his diet was mentioned.

"And John was clothed with camel's hair and with a girdle of skin around his loins; and he did eat locusts and wild honey;" Mark 1:6

John was obviously sustained by the power of God as our nutritionists of today would go crazy over that diet.

John was what the Church needs to be today. A supernatural entity on the earth bringing forth a message from heaven, calling the people back to God without fear or favor, a people being used of God in the way he sees fit. Our prayer should be, never the less, not my will but thy will be done. We must surrender our will to His, because only then will we be properly aligned to God and be able to be used of God to accomplish His divine purpose for our lives.

John born in the comfort of a priest's home, surrounded by the splendor of God represented in the temple, was later transplanted into the wilderness to wait on the Lord so that he could properly serve him. A reed taken from the wetlands, transplanted to a dry place, must have been seen as a crazy plan; but it was God's plan and the people went out to see him. They left the comfort of their houses, towns, religion to go see a man being used of God in a way they had never seen before. He was a spectacle to some, maybe even a gazing stock to others but his message hit home as they all asked in unison:

"What shall we do then?" Luke 3:10

I believe our message is shaped from where we have been. God wants to speak through us to a people lost in sin and heading for a devil's hell, but he wants to take us to the place where he can form his word within us, write it on our hearts, like he wrote it on the tablets of stone for Moses. He took Moses away into a desolate mountain and wrote to him. He no longer wants to write on stones he wants to write his laws in our flesh, so we can be read by men and they will come to see Christ because they saw the message on us.

John was the message, his very presence evoked a spirit of conviction, so much so that Herod put him in prison and later beheaded him in an attempt to clear his conscience.

Are you willing to be used of God? The whole meaning of our lives rests on this question. Are we just concerned about doing our thing, our way, whilst God's plan is put to the side? The Spirit of God is poured out for no other reason but for his people to be full of God so we can be used for his pleasure. John was an example; we need to be the authentic article in our generation. A spectacle for God; out of place by the world's understanding but perfectly positioned by God to wrought a wondrous work that will have generational implications and will bring lasting change.

WASTED ON JESUS

There was an incident in the ministry of Jesus, hardly worth mentioning, you would think, and yet God includes it in three of the Gospels in one form or the other. Mark 14:3-11

"And while he was in Bethany at the home of Simon the leper and reclining at the table, there came a woman with an alabaster vial and poured it over his head. But some were indignantly remarking to one another, "Why has the perfume been <u>wasted</u>? For this perfume might have been sold for over three hundred denarii, and the money given to the poor." And they were scolding her. But Jesus said, "Let her alone; why do you bother her? She has done a good deed to me. For the poor you will always have with you, and whenever you wish, you can do them good; but you do not always have me. She has done what she could; she has anointed my body beforehand for the burial. And truly I say to you wherever the gospel is preached in the whole world, that also which this woman has done shall be spoken of in memory of her." And Judas Iscariot, who was one of the twelve, went off to the chief priest, in order to betray him to them. And they were glad when they

> heard this, and promised to give him money.
> And he began seeking how to betray him at an
> opportune time."

It is not a coincidence that there is a conjunction between the lavish outpouring of this woman and Judas' decision to go to high priest immediately following the incident, to betray Jesus. Jesus said what she had done would be spoken of in memory of her. That is rather exuberant praise and acknowledgement for what seems to men, and even to the disciples of Jesus as a <u>waste.</u>

There are so many things happening in this text, so I chose to label it an incident. It is however very prudent to systematically investigate these different episodes and not only the episodes as a whole but indeed the different characters in the drama.

This incident was not initiated by Jesus as many others were, but by this woman. We know she was used of God because of Jesus' response. In Mark 14:8, Jesus states, the reason for the act, "She hath done what she could; she has anointed my body beforehand for the burial"

Enter The Woman

It is dinner time. The house has the aroma and smell of fresh fruits and vegetables, beans and meats. It must have been a grand occasion as Simon, the once leper is now hosting Jesus. Everybody who is anybody will be there. This must have been one of those events you have to put down on your social calendar. The disciples were there, the elite of society were there. The Gospel of John gives us a clearer insight into the crowd.

John12:9

> "Much people of the Jews therefore knew he was there; and they came not for Jesus' sake only, but that they might see Lazarus also whom he had raised from the dead."

So let us correctly construct the scenario that God had prepared, to use this chosen vessel to perform an act of monumental importance. A dinner party, hosted by a once leper, Simon. In attendance was Jesus' latest miraculous success story – Lazarus. A great throng of people turn up to crash the party, not to see Jesus but to see Lazarus. In the midst of this were the disciples and of course the guest of honor – Jesus.

The Bible stated the timing of her incursion. It must have been significant because the Bible states, "And being in Bethany in the house of Simon the leper, as he sat at meat." Vs. 3, some other verses say when they reclined to dinner. She came at prime time, when everyone was settled for what they thought would be the main event – their dinner, enters this woman. The Gospel of Matthew and Mark do not name her, whilst John calls her Mary. Obviously, her name is not important, but what she did was. Matthew and Mark did not take the time to

29

give her name or family connections which were very important in that day. We read of blind Bartimaeus, son of Timaeus (Mark 10:46) who got healed and set free by Jesus, but have you ever wondered what became of blind Bartimaeus, or of all the persons healed by Jesus. They never did anything useful with their deliverance that we have heard of. Even Lazarus, who was raised from the dead, we don't hear of him pioneering a movement, leading a mighty movement. We see him as a dinner guest. Could it be that God is trying to show us something? Perhaps it is not those who get the blessing that matter but those who give it away, in other words, those who waste their stuff on Jesus.

This woman was not the recipient of a major miracle from Jesus personally, but she was touched by the master that the Holy Spirit was able to use her to perform the burial rites on Jesus by anointing him with all she ever had. Yes, it was all she ever had; Mark declared that it was worth more than a year's wage, her pension. She gave it all she held nothing back. The Bible teaches that she broke the vial. It did not just trickle out, it poured forth. None could be saved and on the other hand none could be lost.

Unlike John the Baptist who was prepared to be used of God from his youth. This woman shows another dimension. A vessel so surrendered to God that at a moment's notice, with no prior thought the Holy Spirit inspiring you into action in the natural, to fulfill an eternal purpose. The blind disciples scoffed at her and asked a question that revealed, for some, how far they were from God's presence. "Why was this waste of the ointment made?"

The Indignant Crowd

Jesus had men around him, that even up to his twilight moment they still did not recognize who he was. Jesus was not blind to those around him. In fact in many cases we are more easily destroyed by those closest to us. One wise man states, 'Gather your leaders around your leg so if one stabs you, you will end up with only a limp. If you put untried and unproven persons too close to your chest the wound might be fatal.'

They were with him daily and it took an unnamed woman to be used to perform one of the most important acts on Jesus before his sacrifice. It brings into sharp focus their motive for being around the Saviour. John 12:9 stated that many people came just to see. Spectators cannot be used of God. They are not committed to the race; they just want to see the next best thing. Too many Christians fit this description in our churches, spectators of God, committed to come to the next viewing called Sunday church, but not committed to Christ. We make the mistake continuously of equating commitment to the work of the ministry to commitment to Christ. As we will discuss later the two couldn't be further apart.

Judas Iscariot was mentioned by John as the disciple who spoke out against the woman. This is significant but it must also be mentioned, flipping back to St. Mark's gospel, that 'there were some that had indignation within themselves.' There were those who had the same thoughts, they were equally as defiled (evil) as Judas. Only Judas had the guts to enunciate what he was thinking. The others hid their iniquity whilst Judas could not hide his, because of who he was.

The act of the woman caused such a stir that it affected not just their minds but it went deep into their subconscious, revealing our hatred of all things heavenly. Even to see someone blessing Christ is offensive to the mindset of the carnal man. They called it a <u>waste</u>.

Mark 14:10-11 ushers us to another step in the episode. Judas' response, after Jesus' validation of the woman's action, and his rebuke, was staggering. Judas went off to the chief priests in order to betray Him.

Jesus response seems to be the straw that broke the camel's back. The very heart of man is revealed here. It seems unnecessary to give so much to Jesus; it could have been used for a better purpose, like feeding the poor and needy. It seems to be more palatable to give money to organizations that feed the poor. It almost seems offensive to lavish your resources on Jesus. You see in this story only Jesus was benefitting from her actions. It did not seem efficient or even sensible when so much more could have been accomplished with this gift. This could not be God, because it was a waste of resources.

It is ironic that this same spirit is in operation today; where giving to a minister or ministry is predicated on the fact that something will be given in return. We are living in the age of investment, when if you give something you expect recompense. Her act was costly because nothing was asked for in return. It made even the disciples recoil in indignation and murmur against the woman, asking, 'For what purpose was this waste.'

We have used doctrines as a broad brush to be applied to every situation. I am referring at this point to the doctrine of sowing and reaping, where it is widely taught that if we sow anything in Christ we must expect an equal or greater return of that thing which we have sown. To add to this we have created a doctrine called 'Fertile Ministries.' So we promote ourselves and tell would be donors what are the benefits of giving to this ministry vs., another. We use the success model, the more successful you are the more donors you can attract. It is even more significant if you have signs and wonders in your ministry, it's an easier sell.

Nothing is wrong with sowing and reaping but God is first not our pet doctrine used to manipulate. It should not be that every cent every moment we give to God is done for our benefit, not his. We have drifted so far away from him. Watchman Nee has said that the principle of waste is the principle of power and we are powerless because we have played it too close to our vest. Jesus loved this woman because, "She has done a good deed to me." God has no respect for the works of men, but he called what this woman did a good deed or work. She came with something very precious and expensive, she came into a room full of men bristling with indignation, but she did not let that deter her. And wherever extravagance for Christ's sake is poured out there will be a corresponding opposition.

There is something lacking in God's Church, namely a pouring out that releases the flow of his life to the unbelieving world. <u>We are antiseptic and correct, but we are not fragrant</u>.[i] This woman was used of God to break the religious stereotype of the mean looking and mean spirited religious type of worshiper, the worshipper who seems to have all the correct answers, but lacks the aroma of the Spirit. She was used to express broken delight before God, holding nothing back. Until we gain the faith to lavish each other with our gifts freely, we run the risk of remaining religious without an intense relationship with God and our fellow saints. Jesus voice is still booming today as it did in the text back then, "Leave the woman alone." The disciples did not understand the value of her worship, nor does the world today. The world wants to restrict us to a worship that trickles; is controlled, manipulated. They are ok with our Sunday morning exuberance, which is limited powerless and palatable.

The moment we decide to bring into worship an extravagance that is beyond the norm of what is taught to be needed or required, we will excite the world to persecute us.

This kind of lavish worship will result in suffering. This type of suffering is redemptive, apocalyptic and will form the process of the imminent return of Christ. This dimension of worship is what Jesus required then and this is what the church needs to walk in now. There is a degree to which the Church is not serving only God. Jesus stated in Matt. 5: "You will be persecuted for my names sake." This strongly suggests that if we are preaching only Jesus it will bring about confrontation with the world. A God Alone vision needs to return to the Church. The early church only preached Jesus and him crucified not psychology. There needs to be a return to a single mindedness of the Church to see Jesus and him alone. This idea is acidic to the world, as the world is more into religious duty than it is into lavishing itself upon Jesus. The early church was greatly persecuted not because they were religious or spiritual; they were ruthlessly hunted down and killed because they preached Jesus. Since Jesus' resurrection the religious order has been trying to silence Him and his true followers. Matt. 28:11-15

"Now when they were going behold, some of the watch came into the city, and showed unto the Chief Priests all the things that were done. And when they were assembled with the elders and had taken counsel they gave large money unto the soldiers, saying, say ye, His disciples came by night, and stole him away while we slept. And if this comes to the Governor's ears, we will persuade him and secure you. So they took the money and did as they were taught: and this saying is commonly reported among the Jews until this day."

Also in the book of Acts chapter 5:40 states-

"And to him they agreed and when they had called the Apostles and beaten them, they commanded that they should not speak in the name of Jesus and then let them go."

All over the New Testament we see where the people of God are persecuted and or go under unusual suffering. Even though their situations might be different there is one common denominator, they all preached or spoke in the name of Jesus. In Matt. 5:11,

"Blessed are ye when men shall revile you and persecute you and say all manner of evil against you falsely, for my name's sake."

There is an absence of persecution because there is a lack of speaking in his name. This is the flashpoint- Jesus.

Jesus further incites religious mockery against the woman by declaring, "And truly I say to you, wherever the Gospel is preached in the whole world, that also which this woman has done shall be spoken of in memory of her."

None of the patriarchs of the faith were given this privilege; her act was to be broadcast all over the world. What seemed a waste to many was of timeless value to God. The apostle Paul writes in 2 Corinthinians4:7, "But we have this treasure in earthen vessels that the Excellency of the power may be of God, and not of us." God is calling us to brokenness, the place of pouring out. There needs to be a total abandon in our worship and service to God. Yes! We will be called radicals, even fanatics, but that was what was required of the Church in her inception and so it shall be in the end. What value do we have to lavish on Jesus, the fragrance of which will change the atmosphere? This will cause a confrontation of cosmic and apocalyptic proportion. Just one act of selfless and sacrificial worship to Jesus has the power to disturb principalities and powers. This woman was used of God in a manner that changed everything we know about worship. Generations after her action is still causing disturbance in the earthly and heavenly realms. This is truly being "Used of God."

BLESSED TO BE BROKEN

Matthew 14:13-21

"When Jesus heard of it, he departed thence by ship into a desert place apart; and when the people had heard thereof, they followed him on foot out of the cities. And Jesus went forth and saw a great multitude and was moved with compassion toward them and he healed their sick.

And when it was evening, his disciples came to him saying this is a desert place, and the time is now past; send the multitude away, that they may go into the villages and buy themselves victuals.

But Jesus said unto them, they need not depart; give ye them food to eat.

And they say unto him we have but five loaves and two fishes.

He said "Bring them hither to me.

And he commanded the multitude to sit down on the grass and took the five loaves and the two fishes, and looking up to heaven he blessed and broke, and gave the loaves to his disciples, and his disciples to the multitude. And they did all eat and were filled: and they took up of the fragments that remained twelve baskets full. And they that had eaten were about five thousand men besides women and children."

The word blessing has undergone severe abuse over the past two decades in church circles. It is a word that I believe needs to be contended for, by every true believer of Christ. It has become a cliché used by people who neither understand its significance nor its value. In fact there has been no word more cheapened than the word blessing. "Bless you brother, bless you sister... bless the Lord etc.

What does it mean to be blessed? What is its importance? As we examine this critical word, I pray that you will desire to be drawn closer to the truth of who Jesus is. The people of God are a blessed people however our definition of being blessed must be derived from a Godly or heavenly perspective and not just an earthly understanding.

I believe that the understanding of the word blessing has eschatological ramifications, as it will greatly affect how the saints of God endure persecution. To misunderstand this word could cause many to fall away as they try to understand God's dealings versus God allowing suffering upon his Church. In fact many books have been written on this one subject over the past decade. A plethora of new ministries have sprung up because of the era of blessings the Church has been going through, especially in the western part of the world. But Jesus' actions in Matthew 14 have greatly impacted my life and will form the foundation of our discourse in this chapter.

The Bible teaches that Jesus blessed the bread and then he broke it and handed it to his disciples to give to the people. Five loaves and two fishes fed over five thousand men not numbering the women and children present. Seen as a major miracle we can get lost in the theatrics of it.

One preacher asked 'When did the miracle take place, in Jesus' hands, in the disciples' hands or when the people received their share? 'Mind boggling question, but we can never tell. There are so many other interesting aspects to the miracle, why there were twelve baskets full left over, what is the significance of the number and so forth. We will not get caught up with those urgent things, let us examine what is important to the Holy Spirit at this time, the principle behind Jesus' action that wrought the miracle.

Brakhah

> Genesis 1:28 "And God blessed them and God said unto them, be fruitful and multiply…"

One of the first acts of God upon creating man was to pronounce or invoke a blessing on him. Similarly, he pronounced a blessing on all the sea creatures and cattle and creeping things, in verse 22 of Genesis chapter one. In both instances the resulting expectation of this blessing was for there to be multiplication, fruitfulness and a filling of their environment. The fish were to fill the sea, the fowls were to fill the air and the cattle the ground and so on. Mankind's expectation however went a lot further as stated in verse 28-:

"And God blessed them and God said unto them, be fruitful and multiply and replenish the earth and subdue it and have dominion over the fish of the sea, over the fowl of the air, and over every living thing that moveth upon the earth."

When God blessed man he was given dominion. In contrast however to the notion of blessing that we are taught today, which is built on the hype of receiving something from God. This notion seems to suggest a lesser type of blessing than the one God invokes.

It seems that God does want to bless mankind, but not so that they can receive something and go away happy, but it seems that true blessings cause man to become something. Man becomes fruitful, he multiplies and he has dominion. What is this constant begging by believers for things pertaining to the basic necessities of life, food, shelter and clothing? It is like a line out of the story of <u>Oliver Twist</u>. The orphan boy, Oliver not being satisfied with his meager meal from his warden, went and asked for more, he said, "Please sir, can I have some more?" and with eyes wide open and nose flaring the warden shouted "More?!… More…! No more!!! Oliver ran back to his seat, totally dejected. This is a picture of the twenty first century Church. We are so lost, that we are living like an orphaned child in an orphanage, not knowing our true Father so we are begging for scraps. Being abused by the wardens some call them Ministers of the Gospel, who come around with words to cause God's children to be in more lack.

No other topic has been more abused by so many for so long. Many starving sickly saints pay out their last dollar to receive a blessing from some snake oil type preacher, prostituting the Word of God and using his anointing for fleshy gain. Scammers, thieves, blasphemers even, they are those that the Bible calls wolves in sheep apparel. But thank God He is restoring his Word, because he has come to be our one true shepherd and redeemer.

God does not want his children to run after **barakh.** He wants us to be **barakh.** God pronounced this over Adam and Eve, they didn't have to look for it they had it. The word blessed, **barakh:- means to be spoken well of**; the Strong's Exhaustive Concordance, further states(pg. 24) **to invoke, to be blessed, to greet.** In Longman's Active Study Dictionary 5th Edition defined blessed as to be lucky and have a special ability or good quality.

I have taken the time to give you these two different renderings of the word blessed to show you how limited both sources, one spiritual and the other intellectual, are in comparison to what God really implies in His Word. The writer Arthur Katz states, "Like all other great Biblical words we can't find a definition for them by reaching for a dictionary. We need rather to be apprehended by the genius of what that word represents.[ii] The genius of what the word represents; oh it's just like Katz to set us straight. We have been living in some lesser reality of God's Word than what he states or even means. There is a theological principle that is called the Law of First Mention, which declares that for you to understand the true meaning of a word or principle you must examine that word or principle in its original instant, where it's original and authentic meaning is known. We have misinterpreted this word and many other Biblical words by superimposing our cultural understanding on words that were spoken from an eternal platform.

Abraham

Let us examine this word a little more, but from a post-fall perspective. God called a man called Abraham; he called him out from his father's house, from his culture, from his value system. God called him out of everything that he was familiar with, and when he responded with

43

obedience, God said, not thought or intimated, so that anyone had to guess later, no God said,

> "And I will make of thee a great nation, and I will bless (**barakh**) thee, and make thy name great; and thou shalt be a blessing: And I will bless them that bless thee, and curse them that curse thee: and in thee shall all families of the earth be blessed. So Abram departed as the Lord had spoken unto him, and Lot went with him: and Abram was seventy –five years old when he departed out of Haran."

Here again when God invoked his blessing on a man, it spoke to an expectation of increase, multiplication that will impact the earth. God declared, "And in thee shall all families of the earth be blessed." Blessings are not something you get, it is a state of being, and it is who you are. Abraham was blessed and from that very moment his entire life was changed. Everything about him was affected by being blessed of God. He left his household, which meant he relinquished his hold on the family fortune as he was the eldest son of Terah; he could only leave with what he had in his matrimonial home. He left the comfort of a well built city to wander in a land that God would later give to his seed as an inheritance, and better still He gave him a heavenly vision of a city whose builder and maker is God. Only a blessed man could be used of God in such a fashion.

Only someone who has the favor of God invoked upon his/her life can withstand the onslaught of worldly men's ridicule, jeers and misunderstanding. Only a blessed man can overcome the inner struggles that would definitely occur because one has decided to be used of God. Abraham was the vessel God chose to use to initiate his redemptive plans for mankind. God's entire intent is summed up in the one phrase,

> "And in thee shall all families of the earth be blessed"

So on the basis of the blessing, Abraham departed out of Haran. Haran a city of well watered springs and palms, an oasis in the wilderness, mountainous and lush, I could easily see why Terah dwelt and died there, it was a type of paradise. It must have taken something greater to cause a man to respond to a living God. Only when God has **barakh** a man can he favor him with brokenness. Brokenness without **barakh** would be grievous and would undoubtedly lead to self-destruction. Abraham could have endured the separation from his family because God had first blessed him and highly favored him.

Genesis 12:5b states

> "Abraham had gathered great substance and souls whilst in Haran."

To give up your source for a heavenly calling shows great faith. The Apostle Paul wrote,

> "Yea doubtless, and I count all things but loss for the Excellency of the knowledge of Christ Jesus My Lord: for whom I have suffered the loss of all things, and do count them but dung that I may win Christ." Philippians 3:8.

The Apostle Paul wrote that he suffered the loss of all things yet he counted all that he suffered, the loss of all things, of little or no value to winning Christ. Such brokenness sounds harsh and painful and I will add in most cases it is. However, brokenness when viewed from a heavenly perspective is something tender, a loving act of God. We will discuss later how it pleased the Father to send his son to the cross. Isaiah 53:10a

> "Yet it pleased the Lord to bruise him."

The saints of God have been running away from brokenness from the beginning of the Church, because we do not understand his ways. We have considered brokenness from a worldly point of view for all our lives. Where we see that when the world breaks you it leaves you crushed and defeated. Brokenness is seen as something to avoid, it is even suggested that if you as a Christian are going through any failure or humiliation in your life you probably are not saved, as blessed people don't go through times of distress. To suffer is taken to mean that you have sin in your life. To encounter misfortune is a sure sign of demonic influence in your life and you need deliverance. The prevailing thought is that God uses brokenness to humble his servant and that could be true in some instances. However, we should never pass judgment on a principle by examining its early stages. The goal of God's breaking is to bring ultimate increase; the Bible has many examples, from beginning to end of men and women who were broken by God who saw great increase and power by the end of their lives. In other words, the process of breaking did not leave God with a bad testimony; on the contrary, those broken by God became those who were greatly used by His Spirit.

The Patriarch Moses, who was blessed by God from birth, the Bible declares,

> "And the women conceived, and bare a son: and when she saw him that he was a <u>goodly</u> child, she hid him three months". Exodus 2:2

He lived forty years before God used the next forty years of his life to break him; to prepare him to be used of God. Not just to lead his people out of Egyptian bondage, but to confront a Pharaoh who believed he was a god. Only a man who was broken by God could have been used of God to dismantle a dynasty such as Pharaoh's. The Bible testifies that Moses was the meekest man who ever lived. (Num 12:3) Coming from being a brash Prince of Egypt, who killed a man and buried him in the sand, who later had to run for his life from the Pharaoh. We found him later at a well in Midian, again fighting for the rights of others who were being unfairly treated. It was in his nature to deliver those who were oppressed, from the Israelites being beaten to now Jethro's sheep herding daughters who were being marginalized by men. He stood up for them and won the favor Jethro, and in time married his eldest daughter. However when we see Moses again in chapter 3 of Exodus, now at the age of eighty years old we find a man broken. Not the brash, confident in his ability person we met forty years earlier, but a man emptied of his own self belief and confidence.

> "And Moses said unto God, who am I, that I should go unto Pharaoh, and that I should bring forth the children of Israel out of Egypt?"

Does this sound like a man who you would choose to lead God's people, all three million of them? Who am I? What a question to ask at this stage of life. It would appear that God will reduce a man down to zero, to rebuild him anew so that he can be used of God. Whilst the devil builds up a man to reduce him to zero in humiliation. His trophy room is littered with so many souls who have been discarded by society because at the height of their earthly achievements they were taken down either by immorality or some other satanic device that was used to ultimately humiliate them and push them into the shadows of history. Some of these once powerful men even took their own lives when they saw what they were reduced to.

Peter vs. Judas Iscariot

Peter and Judas two men, both disciples of Jesus their lives call for examination based on how each was used. On the same night both experienced brokenness, humiliation, guilt, and defeat. However, both men did not end up the same way. One eventually was increased fifty days later, whilst the other took his own life by the end of the night.

As we examine these two lives, it will become evident to you that your level of submission to God is vitally important. Judas Iscariot teaches us that you can be around God, the anointing or even the best the church has to offer and still remain unchanged. We must submit our lives totally to Christ or we will end up confused like Judas. Having good intentions, he wanted to see Messiah come in all his glory and rescue his blessed people, nothing is wrong with that however; his mind was not impacted or changed by the ministry of Jesus. So he still harbored thoughts of a Messianic War fought between Jesus and their oppressors, the Romans. The words of Jesus did not pierce his soul, words like

"I came to seek that which was lost." Matt 18:11 or

"For God sent not his Son into the world to condemn the world; but that the world through him might be saved." John3:17; he also reiterated at another point.

"But go rather to the lost sheep of the house of Israel" Matthew 10:6

There were countless other times when Jesus made reference to his mission here on earth, yet this had no impact on Judas' preconceived notion of the mission of Jesus. This reluctance to bend ones will to serve the Lord made him a prime target to be used by Jesus' arch enemy, Lucifer. What was true of Judas back then is true of us today. Our unwillingness to yield our will to the Holy Spirit makes us unusable to God, and places us in the category of being an enemy of God. As Jesus states,

"He that is not with me is against me; and he that gathered not with me scattereth abroad." Matthew 12:30

To be used of God we must go through the process of daily surrendering to Christ. Anything that is left of us will become a threat to us. Judas was given the perfect opportunity to die to himself, when he encountered the woman with the alabaster box. He should have joined her in praising Jesus; but he became indignant with her act because he saw a better use for it: to line his own pocket. The writer John editorialize his eye witness account by revealing the true heart intentions of Judas:-

"Then saith one of his disciples, Judas Iscariot, Simon's son which should betray him. Why was this not this ointment sold for three hundred pence and given to the poor? This he said not that he cared for the poor; but because he was a thief, and had the bag, and bear what was put there in." John 12:4-6

Judas is the antithesis to loud mouth, ever talking, rebuking Peter. We rarely hear from Judas. He appears from the outside to be the perfect disciple, not a trouble maker, well reasoned and quite intelligent. Yet at the Passover he was handpicked by Satan to betray his Lord.

"Now the feast of unleavened bread drew nigh, which is called the Passover. And the chief priests and scribes sought how they might kill him; for they feared the people.

Then entered Satan into Judas surnamed Iscariot, being of the number of the twelve." Luke 22:1-3

Judas was not a wicked person by definition; he could not be compared to Hitler, or some other great warriors of the past who wrought wickedly. Other than being accused of being a thief, we know little of the man that Satan decided to enter, himself, to make sure that Jesus was crucified as scheduled. Consider this, in the drama playing out before us; there were other key persons in the plot, who I thought it would have been more important for Lucifer himself to enter. For example, Pontius Pilate, Caiaphas the high priest, the persons sent to make lying accusations against Jesus, even the soldiers in charge of the crucifixion.

These persons, I believe were more critical in the drama and how they played their role would have made it happen or not. Satan did have a great influence on them all, however for the gospel writer to make mention of that one event is significant, Satan entered Judas.

Let us pause for a moment and recall the purpose of this book, Being Used of God. We are endeavoring to establish a critical argument/ revelation on the importance of being used of God and the care that God takes in selecting those in whom he decides to dwell and to use to carry out his plans. We have already examined John the Baptist who was selected, prepared and then unleashed on his generation and his voice is still as strong today as it was then. We have looked at the woman who interrupted the dinner party at the house of the leper and how she was used of God to ultimately change the course of worship itself. How men who were full of religious pride were indignant and wrought at her worship. How she was used of God mightily!

Now here is my clincher. Why did Satan seemingly only possess Judas for the event? He chooses to use Judas personally in the unfolding of the drama. Could it be that we have underestimated the role of Judas in this scenario. He must have been prepared by Satan to be used of him in such a fashion. Judas understanding the gravity of his actions went out afterwards and killed himself, opting for death over living a life with this mark against him. If Satan chooses whom he uses so carefully, how much more will God. God desires to use us for his Glory, he is processing us everyone in a different way, but we are all being processed for one purpose – to be used of God.

Judas must have believed he was doing the right thing, for him to go along with the satanic plot to kill his master and friend. If you understand this you could see why it was not difficult for Judas to be used in this manner. He was believed to be of the group called the zealots, who were a religious sect in Israel at the time who wanted to see the coming of Messiah. They were devoted men just like the apostle Paul was. He was trained undoubtedly from a youth to think in violent terms against their gentile oppressors, who were the Romans. So his training would prepare him to do anything for the liberation of his people from the Roman gentiles.

Hence it is not inconceivable to consider with Brother Judas that if Jesus is truly the Messiah, which he must be, then if provoked or even threatened with death, Jesus would manifest his true Messianic nature and become the savior they all wanted, even Judas. The Savior of the Jews that I believe was Judas' true intent and so betrayal was only a means to an end.

He was thinking in an earthy and natural way, only taking into consideration what he could see. Paul teaches us, that the carnal mind is at enmity with God (Romans 8:7). Judas like Cain was earthy, only minding the things of the natural, "but the natural man receiveth not the things of the Spirit of God: for they are foolishness unto him: neither can he know them, because they are spiritually discerned." 1 Corinthians 2:14.

When Judas finally discerned what he had been used to do he tried to undo it by returning the thirty pieces of silver and he said, "I have sinned in that I have betrayed the innocent blood. And they said what is that to us? See thou to that. And he cast down the pieces of silver in the temple, and departed and went out and hanged himself." Matthew 27: 4-5. This tragic lesson shows us that if we do not allow Christ to break us the world's system of breaking will ultimately destroy us. Judas had an opportunity to bow his heart like the woman with the alabaster box, but his stubbornness led him down a path that cost him his life.

KEFA

The Apostle Peter was the antithesis of Judas. He was as stubborn and opinionated, confident and very self assured. Unlike Judas who went away quietly, the last time we heard and saw Peter before that faithful night, he was publicly making strong declarations about his love and commitment to Jesus.

> "And he said unto him Lord. I am ready to go with thee, both into prison, and to death." Luke 22:33

Just before the breaking of Luke 22:31-end there was an account in Matthew's gospel chapter 16:17, when Jesus stated publicly over Peter,

> "And Jesus answered and said, Blessed art thou, Simon bar Jonah…"

Jesus blessed Peter, the Greek word used was *makarios* which describes the state of the believer, a blessed person is one whom God makes fully satisfied; not because of favorable circumstances, but because he indwells the believer through Christ. The one who receives the blessing is the one who is in the world yet independent of the world, this is the kind of blessing that Christ offers, not this earthly counterfeit blessing we so parade today as God's best for his children. Kefa (Peter) could only have survived his brokenness on the strength of this blessing received from Christ. If Peter needed it, so do we today, let's seek out God's true blessing that only comes from heaven. The Bible states, Jesus "looked up to the heavens" Matthew 14:19-21, this blessing comes from heaven.

In the Luke 22 scripture Jesus was speaking to Peter and he interrupted the Lord; Peter was a man in his prime, what the Lord was telling him of these things could not be,

> "And the Lord said Simon, Simon, behold Satan hath desired to have you, that he may sift you as wheat;" Luke 22:31

In this very chapter Satan had entered Judas (Luke 22 vs. 3). Two attempts one successful entry. Both men would have experienced defeat and failure that night, but Jesus continued...

> "But I have prayed for thee that thy faith fails not: and when you are converted, strengthen thy brethren." Luke 22:32

To this Peter replied he was ready to die for the Lord, and Lord replied,

> "I tell thee, Peter, the cock shall not crow this day before that thou shalt thrice deny that thou knowest me." Luke 22:34

Kefa had to go through his crucible of fire before he was considered ready to be used of God. He was initially to strengthen his brethren. By the end of the night, this brash, confident man was perfectly reduced to a vessel that God could use. The man who stood up on the day of Pentecost was not self assured, but was Spirit-led. He was not wise in the things of this world, but he stood as a man sent from heaven speaking with authority that caused all to stop and listen. Only a vessel blessed then broken by God could be used to impact so many persons in just one moment. The Bible declared that over three thousand persons responded to the gospel message from Kefa that day.

The rest of his life showed forth a spirit of humility and grace that he did not possess before being broken. We recount the incident between the Apostle Paul and Peter in Galatia where Paul publicly rebuked him over a matter. Galatians 2:11-14. The Apostle Peter showed how changed he was as he submitted to counsel and later in his letter in 2Peter 3:15 he stated

> "And account that the long suffering of our Lord is salvation; even as our beloved brother Paul also according to the wisdom given unto him hath written unto you."

Peter addressed Paul as his beloved brother, there was no animosity or pride even though he had been publicly humiliated by the Apostle, he humbled himself and showed respect and love for the Apostle Paul, such maturity, such brokenness. Too much of the good in us cannot be used by God because it is rooted and founded in self which is in turn rooted in the tree of the knowledge of good and evil. Self promotion, self gratification and self preservation are all too important in the world today even in the Church. However, it is the process of breaking that gives increase in God. It might not feel good being broken, but brokenness carries with it eternal value.

Jesus blessed the bread them he broke it and handed it to his disciples. God is after something in our lives, yes he wants to bless us and he already has, but be wants to break us now. Our flesh will resist the breaking but that is rooted in self preservation. Jesus said

> "Verily, verily I say unto you. Except a corn of wheat fall into the ground and die, it abideth alone: but if it dies it bringeth forth much fruit". John 12:24

When the seed falls to the ground and dies, the outer shell is finally broken and life bursts forth from one seed. The result is the multiplication of that one seed into an ear of corn. Brokenness brings multiplication. Satan knows this; hence he has been working very hard among the saints to have us flee from brokenness.

So we end up with a Church body that is still largely unusable in the hand of God.

We must revisit our faulty foundations of Christian teachings on brokenness. Most Christian doctrine on brokenness, teach that God breaks the saints then rewards them with blessings. This couldn't be further from the truth as Jesus is the only reward of the saints. We are not encouraged by the apostles or even Jesus to seek after blessing. The Bible declares that they are yea and amen. However, the Church in most recent history has gone overboard on this teaching on blessing that does not recognize the need for deeper things, such as brokenness. This is the plan of God, to break us after he has invoked a heavenly blessing on us so we can bring forth his glory. Submit to his loving plan for you today and watch how God can use you to change many lives.

Later in this book I will discuss the lives of several persons who were broken by God but were used to feed thousands, and though some of them have passed on into eternity, their lives are still feeding many. There is no greater joy, no greater call than to be used of God. Let us humble ourselves under the mighty hand of God and let him increase us, not just with earthly wealth and things which will come our way but let him increase us with heavenly things, treasures that cannot rust or be stolen. Let him bless us so when the breaking comes it will not be grievous, but we can say like the Apostle Paul in 2 Corinthians 4:17

> "For our light affliction, which is but for a moment worketh for us a far more exceeding and eternal weight of glory."

Only when we allow God to bless us then break us can we confess with Paul, that an affliction is light and but for a moment. Paul was stoned, shipwrecked three nights, beaten, imprisoned for the gospel and called this entire thing, light affliction. He knew who he was his state of being, he was blessed regardless of his earthly situation, and he counted it all joy to lose all to win Christ. This position of one of the founding fathers of our faith must also be our position for our lives to have any relevance.

There is an increase that only comes after you are broken. It does not come because you are anointed, you are intelligent or graced. It will only come because you were broken. To be used of God to affect the lives of countless numbers of persons can only come after you are broken.

There is a move of God coming and it involves the same old thing. He is getting ready to bless us so he can finally break his Church and bring forth many more sons and daughters of God for his end time harvest.

THE SUFFERING SERVANT OUR REIGNING KING

"Yet it pleased the Lord to bruise him, he hath put him to grief..." Isaiah 53:10

In all of scripture, the fifty second and third chapters of the book of Isaiah has given Jewish scholars the most trauma. It has caused a great struggle within Judaism because it clearly connects the Messiah with suffering and death. It is hard for the Jews to see their Messiah as being defeated since his earthly entry will have a global impact. Therefore it is not hard understand the Jewish scholar's dilemma, so the obvious solution was to suggest two Messiah's, one who would suffer and another who would reign. This goes contrary to the teaching of the Torah. They could not foresee how Jesus (the Messiah) could fulfill both sets of prophecies.

To be used of God to do wonderful miracles, to help the poor and needy never seems to cause any ripples in life's continuous smooth stream. However, when words like suffering, pain, misfortune and even death are associated with God's purpose for mankind; all kinds of unsettling emotions are unleashed. These Jewish scholars were prepared to change the prophecy, because they could not bring themselves to see their Messiah being used of God in a fashion that even suggest defeat. The Bible is loud in its pronouncement,

"Yet it pleased the Lord to bruise him,"

What?!!! This must be a mistranslation, the work of evil men trying to bring the scriptures into disrepute. This does not show God in a favorable light. It pleased him to bruise, his only begotten son. But in the Jewish understanding Messiah cannot be harmed, even worse Messiah cannot die. He is our champion. We can just imagine the turmoil in Judaism over these words. But God was serious, Jesus was submitted and history has been impacted eternally because of how the Son was used by the Father.

The Father's Plan

"And all things are of God, who hath reconciled us to himself by Jesus Christ, and hath given to us the ministry of reconciliation.

To wit, that God was in Christ, reconciling the world unto him, not imputing their trespasses unto them; and hath committed unto us the word of reconciliation." 2 Corinthians 5:18-19

In regard to the life, death, burial and resurrection of Jesus Christ, the Bible uses very strong imagery. He is referred to as the Lion of the tribe of Judah

(Revelations 5:5) He is called the bright and morning star; (Revelations 22:16) He is understood as being the captain of the host of heaven (Joshua 5:14-15). Many other glowing terms are used in scripture to describe the awesomeness of Jesus; however none of those aforementioned or understood have more power or eternal weight than Lamb of God.

This term, a seemingly simple form, sums up the Father's Plan for his son in his eternal perspective. The imagery is so powerful it turns up in the Revelation of Jesus in chapter 5:6

> "And I beheld, and lo in the midst of the throne and of the four beasts, and in the midst of the elders stood a lamb…"

John the Baptizer was the first one to announce him publicly.

> "The next day John seeth Jesus coming unto him and saith, "Behold the Lamb of God, which taketh away the sins of the world!" John1:29

Jesus was introduced in his public ministry as the Lamb of God. I am taking my time on this point as I want you to understand what the Holy Spirit is ministering to you at this time. The fact that the imagery of the lamb was used is significant and bears further investigation. A lamb as defined by the Oxford English Dictionary is a young sheep. They were bred for just one purpose to be used as food, in other words to be killed. In the Jewish culture where we find Jesus the lamb also had other important uses, they were used as sacrifices, mainly sin sacrifices and for priestly anointing. So to identify Jesus as a lamb clearly positioned him as a sacrifice. It was the Father's original plan to use Jesus, his only begotten son as the ultimate sacrifice for our sins. Let us wrap our minds around this for just a moment. The sacrificing process is one of the most horrific things you could ever witness. The Bible calls it a slaughter. The Book of Leviticus teaches us in gory details the practice of offering up a sacrifice.

The animal's throat is cut, when the blood gushed out it was caught in a basin; the carcass was then cut open from neck to sternum. The innards were burnt as an offering that is the liver, fat, kidneys and the fat thereof. The rest of the animal was cut up and offered as a part of the burnt sacrifice. The dung however was discarded outside the camp to be burnt. Leviticus 9:3-:

> "And unto the children of Israel thou shalt speak saying; take ye a kid of the goats for a sin offering; and a calf and a lamb, both of the first year, without blemish for a burnt offering."

God went to great lengths to detail to Moses the specific type of sacrifice he required, even how it must be done. It must have been a bloody ritual, perhaps very difficult to stomach.

This we were taught was a foreshadow of the one true sacrifice, which was foretold would come and wipe away the sins of the world. So when John identified Jesus as the one, we must bring ourselves, even for a moment to understand what the heavenly realms were going through as the reality of Jesus' mission was now clear for everyone to see and possibly understand. Matthew 1:21 declares

"...call his name Jesus for he shall save his people from their sins."

Why A Sacrifice?

The question must be asked here, Why a sacrifice? How does this act seem to appease God and bring man back into alignment with his creator? The word sacrifice is first mentioned immediately after the expulsion of Adam and Eve from Eden and next immediately after the flood. These stories illustrate the nature of sin and its consequences. Adam and Eve suffered a spiritual death by being separated from God. In Noah's day most of the human race had died in the flood, only the soothing aroma of Noah's sacrifice changed God's attitude so that he promises never to destroy creation again Genesis 8:20-21.

In the trial of Abraham before God in Genesis 22, God gave us further insight into his plans to use his Son as the ultimate sacrifice. When Abraham prophetically declared to his own son:-

> "And Abraham said, my son, God will provide himself a lamb for a burnt offering: so they went both of them together" Genesis 22:8

They both went together suggest such confidence, such unity of purpose. Isaac was old enough to resist his father but he went along, because faith was generated by him, through those words. He was no longer concerned about where the sacrifice was because he could clearly identify the wood and the fire. Isaac wasn't just being the obedient son, he was living by faith in God whose words must be trusted or there is no hope. He allowed his father to go as far as tying him to the altar and raising the knife...knowing full well that if God did not come through he was dead.

We preach much about the faith of Abraham to go along with God's plan, and he deserves all the accolades he has gotten, but we too often forget to mention the role of the son in this drama. He was used of God just as much as his father and I believe if we come to understand Isaac's act of obedience to pay the ultimate sacrifice we can understand Jesus' heart towards his father.

We must understand that Jesus came to this earth with a promise from his Father that he would raise him up after three days of being dead. Jesus had to trust his Father's word. But Jesus went further he states, "I and my father are one." This could only mean that Jesus *not only agreed with his Father's will, he helped to craft it. Thus he is not only the suffering servant, but he is the submissive son.* Who for the joy set before him endured the cross, despising the shame, and is set down at the right hand of the throne of God. (Hebrews 12:2) He counted the cost and yet still he endured.

God is looking for a church that will count the cost of her suffering and still decide to go through with it for the joy which is set before her. We must break free from the world's appetite for immediate gratification and lock ourselves into a more holy perspective... a heavenly perspective. If the Church of the Living God does not come to this type of thinking soon, we will not be able to be used of God in the ways he intended, so as to bring judgment upon Satan and his works on the Earth.

This lack of an eternal, heavenly perspective has made most of the body weak and susceptible to continual spiritual failure. We are still stuck at the level of the temptation of Christ in Matthew 4:1-11. The enemy tempted Jesus three times with things that could give immediate gratification to his flesh. Turn stones to bread to alleviate your real hunger, yes Jesus change the nature of and purpose of a thing to suit your fleshy desires no matter how genuine it is. Jesus response was that man must not live by bread alone but by every word that proceedeth from the mouth of God. Yes, my body is writhing in pain from not eating for forty days, but I am being sustained by the word of my God. Paul teaches us in 2 Corinthians 4:16

> "For which cause we faint not; but though our outward man perish, yet the inward man is renewed day by day."

Are you being sustained by God's daily word, or are you living from your own efforts of turning stone into bread. The need was legitimate but the process of satisfying the need would have been satanic. It is satanic and devilish to superimpose your will upon another for your own benefit. Stones have a purpose and it is not to be made into bread. God is putting his finger on our selfish ambitions. Good things in the world's eyes but a distraction with fatal consequences to the things of God. How many times have we manipulated a situation or even a person to get ahead? It might have seemed legitimate at the time, but our impatience with God shouts loudly to him saying, I will trust my own way over yours.

Satan went for the greatest need in Jesus' life then to tempt him to sin. He will do the same with us today. If Jesus was controlled by his senses, by his carnal desires he would not have survived this ordeal, and we will not survive either if we are controlled by our carnal desires, no matter how basic they are, we will be exploited and then defeated. The third temptation was also cruel, the tempter offered Jesus all the kingdoms of the world, truly at that point it was his (Satan's) to give. If Jesus was caught up in his carnal nature he could reason it out… all the "good" he could accomplish **NOW.** He didn't have to go to the cross he could have immediate rule. What had been promised by the Father as a future event in Jesus' life, that would necessitate him going through the death of the cross and only after resurrection would he be ready to rule and reign at his right hand, Satan was masterfully offering it to him **NOW.** Jesus was able to resist the tempter because he had a heavenly perspective. He knew from whence he came and who he served. Jesus' reply:

> "Get thee hence, Satan for it is written, thou shalt worship the Lord thy God and him only shalt thou serve." Matthew 4:10 KJV

We serve a heavenly cause first and foremost in our lives, our direction comes from heaven. We are not of this earth; we must see ourselves as sojourners and pilgrims in this world. Our vision must be that of Abraham who looked for a city with foundations whose builder and maker is God. This kind of perspective is critical to our victory in these last days. Jesus was able to overcome the temptation by having his focus fixed on the word and his Father, to the detriment of his body, yet he was able to prevail and went on to be used of God to the redeeming of mankind. The Apostle John put it succinctly,

"For all that is in the world, the lust of the flesh, and the lust of the eyes, and the pride of life…"
(1John 2:16)

The enemy will weave his temptation web from these three power roots.

Only those who have put to death their carnal nature can be effectively used of God and only they will receive his reward. Just a reminder here, there is no reward for being saved. Yes you will go to heaven, but only those who do the works of God will be rewarded, when their works are judged by fire they will stand the test because it will be pure gold. There is a call for the Church to be matured in this age, she must push past her adolescence and strive to grow. The gifts of the Holy Spirit are given for just this purpose, for the Church to become mature.

In the days of King Nebuchadnezzar of Babylon, before a person could serve in his court, they had to go through years of preparation and training, as we saw in Daniel. So if to be used by a heathen King took so much preparation and time, why should God settle for our lame acts of immature service?

The Passover Context

Five days before the Passover, the day that the lamb was selected to be slain to atone for the sins of the household. The lamb was to be selected and brought into the house to be inspected. For five days the lamb was examined by the head of the household to see if there was any blemish or impurity in it. God instructed Moses:-

"Speak to all the congregation of Israel, saying, on the tenth day of the month they were each one to take a lamb for themselves according to their father's household, a lamb for each household. And you shall keep it until the fourteenth day of the same month." Exodus 12:3-6

This was a prophecy that Jesus, the true Passover lamb, would come to fulfill, as it was true for the literal lambs so too for Jesus as he entered Jerusalem five days before his crucifixion. He did this, perfectly fulfilling the word of God. While he was entering the city the ritual Passover lambs were themselves being taken into the houses. As the lambs would have been examined for disqualifying flaws, so the scribes, Pharisees and Sadducees were challenging Jesus trying to find a flaw in him, none was found. He was the acceptable sacrifice for God's Passover. The earthly rulers on their part however resigned themselves hiring false witnesses against him.

In John19:42, we note that Jesus was slain on the Jewish day of preparation. On this day all Passover lambs were slain to prepare for the feast. As Jesus was nailed to the cross, knives were being put to the throat of sacrificial lambs. The fulfillment of the type was taking place in their midst.

> "Surely he hath borne our griefs and carried our sorrows: yet we did esteem him stricken, smitten of God and afflicted." Isaiah 53:4

He was the acceptable sacrifice for our Passover once and for all. Jesus like Isaac surrendered to the will of his Father because he loved his Father and trusted him. These are two key tools everyone who desires to be used of God must possess. We must love God and we must trust him. Without this foundation we would be tossed in the winds of our folly without rest, as we try to please God in our own strength. We must love God. This means that we must come from the presupposition that in all things pertaining to me, God has my best interest at heart and will do nothing to my harm unless it is necessary. **The bride of Christ today wrestles with the issue of God's love as she has permanently tied his love to his giving of gifts. So she cannot see how afflictions could be part of God's plan for her maturity.** Hence certain words are glossed over in the Bible as not relevant to the Church in this age. However I recall the words of God clearly where he states: -

> "For whom the Lord loveth he **chasteneth**" (Hebrews 12:6)

He went further to declare-:

> "That the trail of your faith, being much more precious than gold that perisheth, though it be tried with fire, might be found unto praise and honor and glory at the appearing of Jesus Christ." 1 Peter 1:7

Also:-

> "He that hath an ear let him hear what the Spirit saith unto the churches; to him that **overcometh** will I give to eat of the tree of life which is in the midst of the paradise of God." Revelation 2:7

Furthermore:-

> "Confirming the souls of the disciples, and exhorting them to continue in the faith, and that we must through much **tribulation** enter into the Kingdom of God." Acts 14:22

I don't want to exhaust you with these scriptures, but you may never have read these verses in your Holy Bible. God requires one response from his chosen vessels, he requires our love. A love rooted in a trust is impregnable. The original disciples all went to their death with a level of boldness. Art Katz wrote, "There are saints who actually went with rejoicing to the stake to be burned alive. They saw it as the logic, the conclusion and the verification of their true faith.[iii] To be used of

God in this way, oh the blessing, the peace, the power. Those saints must have been ridiculed by society and their unsaved peers, yet with joy they endured great suffering even choosing death over serving any other king. God's eulogy of them is found in Hebrews 11:38a

"Of whom the world was not worthy:"

They were rewarded with a heavenly home because they rejected all the world had to offer. We will look more closely at this verse in Hebrews in the later chapters.

The writer of Hebrews further illustrated the point:-

"But call to remembrance the former days, in which after ye were illuminated ye endured a great fight of afflictions; Partly, whilst ye were made a gazingstock both by reproaches and afflictions; and partly whilst you became companions of them that were so used.

For you had compassion of me in my bonds, and took joyfully the spoiling of your goods, knowing in yourself that ye have in heaven a better and an enduring substance." Hebrews 10:32-34

The Bible clearly shows us that these precious saints were afflicted and made a gazing stock and this came after they were illuminated by the word of God. Additionally, they took joyfully the spoiling of their goods not just begrudgingly or with great remorse. They endured their affliction with joy. They were used of God as a laughing stock, that was His plan and the saints went along with it… with joy! History records that the world was turned upside down by this generation; the gospel covered the entire known world at that time. There were no satellites, telephones or mega-churches, just a handful of saints who loved the Lord more than their own lives and so were used of God to change and impact the culture of the whole world. The Church required people like that then, we certainly require saints like that today.

Our Reigning King

"Which he wrought in Christ, when he raised him from the dead, and set him at his own right hand in the heavenly places,

Far above all principality, and power, and might, and dominion, and every name that is named, not only in this world, but also in that which is to come:" Ephesians 1:20-21

It was God in Christ reconciling the world to himself and it was God who raised him from the dead, and set him at his own right hand in heavenly places, when we see him again he will not be a suffering servant but, he will be a reigning King. When John saw him during the revelation he fell as dead at the sight of King Jesus, eyes like fire, shining like the sun. We will be like him. Yes! We will shine like the sun, we will reign, but only after we have served the purpose of the Father.

Jesus was given a seat that placed him far above principality, powers and dominions in this world and the one which is to come. Jesus has been given all power because he made the ultimate sacrifice. We are also called to sacrifice; daily we must allow the Holy Spirit to use us as the Father prescribes, for his pleasure. We must have the same attitude as Jesus, which the Apostle Paul described:

> "Who, being in the form of God, thought it not robbery to be equal with God:
>
> But made himself of no reputation, and took upon him the form of a servant and was made in the likeness of men:" Phillipians2:6-7

Are we willing to take off our puny veneer of self importance and allow God to strip us down to the point where he can use us? Too many of us are too full to be used of God. We need to allow the Holy Spirit to search us and empty us out of all the things that would impede our relationship with God. Let us lay aside the sin. What is sin? Everything that separates us from God is sin. Let us become like a lamb, gentle, humble and usable. So that God can accomplish his eternal purpose through us. With Jesus as our High

Priest and standard, we are perfectly positioned to hear from God.

You are a choice vessel, meet for the master's use, let this mind be in you which was also in Christ!

THE TRUE ANOINTING

Her voice was the defining sound for her generation. Her seemingly well choreographed moves across the stage at the Shrine Auditorium were hypnotic as they were rhythmic. Her voice seemed to boom, in a silky kind of way, drawing in every attendee to the meeting into a rapturous gaze. She was not loud, nor brash, she never screamed; petite in form but a giant in the spirit, one of God's Generals.

The time: The late 1960's,

The place: Los Angeles,

Every month for a decade, it was standing room only as Jesus wrought astounding miracles by the hand of Kathryn Kuhlman. The world was astonished, media houses fought for the privilege to talk to her. Yet she never lost her passion, her humility, or her fire.

Yes! There were many others in what seemed to be the golden era of the Church gone by. Men like David Wilkerson, who was preaching at the Melody land Theater every month, would see nights when over a thousand souls would be mightily converted. Oral Roberts would see his tents filled night after night as Jesus would turn up and show himself strong to a nation steeped in New Age thoughts and Science. Man stepped on the moon for the first time, God released the Charismatic revival that defined a generation. A great awakening was sweeping the western world. God was using great orators like A.W. Towzer to expound on Biblical truths that baffled the minds and convicted their souls; Pentecost was happening all over again. Evangelist Billy Graham, Billy Sunday, Jack Coe to name a few were household names. There were also ordinary housewives, blue-collar workers, school teachers, doctors who were used of God to perform great miracles in their daily lives. Some of these stories will be mentioned later. Truly this was a golden era, with all those names mentioned and countless others that we have not, I choose just for this moment to zero in on Miss Kathryn Kuhlman.

Miss Kuhlman was truly anointed by God to impact her generation, through the gift of miracles signs and wonders. Yet, I fear she must be horrified at what is being purveyed as the anointing today. Evangelist Mario Murillo, sums up my feelings well, he stated, "What a presence of God followed that woman! These were meetings with violent miracles in an atmosphere of dignity. Now we have violent meeting but few miracles. All who believe today that they have inherited her mantle should be quiet! There are still many of us who remember her anointing"[iv]

His words are pungent, there are still many of us who remember her anointing. What is called the Anointing today is nothing more than a freak show in many cases, people push down victims on the platform, after they set someone to catch them. One popular preacher of the 90's would act like he was shooting people down with his fingers, even going between his legs or behind him and the people would be slain in the spirit. When this was done the crowd would go wild with excitement, as bodies upon bodies would be heaped upon each other as a prize for the anointing on show.

The gimmicks, the theatrics all were employed to keep our audiences coming back for more. The real and the genuine were being replaced by the profane and entertaining. To further compound this lie and to keep God's people under oppression, many books and articles were written during this time (80-90's), calling into question the life of many of our heroes of the Charismatic revival. Kathryn Kuhlman was not spared, as the enemy went after seemingly minor, confessed and reputed failings of our human heroes. A self righteousness was formed and arrogant preachers were now emerging from everywhere, speaking great words, swaying the masses, again, whilst the truly anointed vessels were pushed to the back of the proverbial bus.

We forget that God uses broken and marred vessels; our heroes should not be worshipped just respected. But we have neither respected nor honored our founding fathers because we believe we are better. But there are still many of us who remember their anointing. We are in a time where what is truth is skewed, truth is relative, subjective even. Truth is no longer viewed as absolute. We are in a dangerous time.

Our neglect of the past is now showing itself in ways that are frightening at best. The scripture is being viewed and interpreted mostly through the lens of contemporary ideology. Many precious Biblical terminologies are being trampled upon by our new thought. One such term that requires rescuing is "The Anointing". With the back drop of the last global move of God, the Charismatic Renewal, we will piece together the broken term identified as the Anointing and we will restore it to the consciousness of those who would be used of God.

Throw The Baby Out With The Bath Water

It would be ludicrous to see someone throwing out their baby with the bath water and remain silent. But this is what has been taking place. The human frailties of our fallen champions of the faith have been used by today's generation of preachers to totally neglect the life and important teachings of that preceding generation. We look to our success and influence as evidence of our greater state of affairs over our predecessors life of sometimes poverty or not having a great material legacy to pass on to this generation. Yes; let me quickly note that not all were so unfortunate, we still have the legacy of great hospitals, Bible Colleges and even communities established during the 60's and beyond.

However I am not so concerned about their material legacy, I am more troubled about the potential to be lost to a generation if we do not take drastic actions now to revisit the paths our forefathers pioneered for us. Their names are all but forgotten and so too their mighty acts. Lester Sumrall, Howard Carter, Leonard Ravenhill, names that brought great fear in the kingdom of darkness, are all but forgotten. Their anointing however lives on because Christ was their anointing.

Their lives in many cases were spotless and full of integrity, used of God to subdue nations and conquer spirits. Their stories must be freshly rehearsed in our hearing so that we can stand on the shoulders of giants to slay our giants. These men and women walked in the anointing. They valued the anointing so it was seen as sacred, not to be trampled upon not to be trifled with. They were seen as weird, too serious about life, 'too holy'. They were declared to be too heavenly minded thus they were no earthly good. On the contrary the earth rocked and shook under their watch. Presidents consulted with them, cities were conquered by them in Jesus' name and as a new generation desperate to see God's hands we cry where are the miracles of our fathers. **We must stop now, repent of our gross arrogance and learn from these champions, if nothing else, what we should not do when we are anointed**. Aimee Simple McPherson, Fanny-Mae Crosby, Mother Theresa, and their lives must become required reading for this generation if we are to survive.

The Anointing Oil

In the book of Exodus, under the instructions given by the Lord to Moses concerning the Tabernacle of Moses, we have specific directions pertaining to this holy oil.

> "Take thou also unto thee principal spices, of pure myrrh five hundred *shekels,* and of sweet cinnamon half so much, *even* two hundred and fifty *shekels,* and of sweet calamus two hundred and fifty *shekels,*
>
> And of cassia five hundred *shekels,* after the shekel of the sanctuary, and of oil olive an hin:
>
> And thou shalt make it an oil of holy ointment, an ointment compound after the art of the apothecary: it shall be an holy anointing oil.
>
> And thou shalt anoint the tabernacle of the congregation therewith, and the ark of the testimony" Exodus 30:23-26

To fully understand the concept of the anointing, we must come to grips with its function when originally mentioned. In the aforementioned text we see that great pains were taken to design and acquire the Anointing oil. God was specific in detailing the ingredients to be used to Moses. This detail was not just the ingredients but also the specific amounts. Each ingredient had a special purpose, each one was quite valuable. We have devalued the anointing today because we do not understand how costly it is. Let us briefly study each ingredient before we define the term, Anointing.

Pure Myrrh

Myrrh is a resin (gum) that oozes from a tiny shrub. Although it was very bitter to the taste, it produced a fragrance so pleasing that it had great value in Biblical times. The word myrrh literally means bitter.

Sweet Cinnamon

The cinnamon tree smells offensive, but the bark is sweet. This was not widely grown so it was expensive and precious.

Sweet Calamus

Calamus was a tall reed that grew in the hostile environment of miry-clay. The word literally means, 'a branch or reed'.

Cassia

Like cinnamon, cassia is found in the bark of a shrub. It grows in high altitudes and possesses a little purple flower. Biblically the root of the word means bowing down or shriveled, as in bowing before the Lord in reverent worship. It has a unique smell, greatly sought after and bore seasonally high in the mountains.

Olive Oil

The olive oil was the ingredient that bound all the spices together. This blending together of sweet and bitter speaks of the unity involved in the holy anointing of the Lord upon his ministers.

The Anointing was so precious before God, that if anyone made it for their own personal use they would be put to death. Another important instruction was that the anointing oil should not be poured upon man's flesh, or upon a stranger.

> "Upon man's flesh shall it not be poured, neither shall ye make any other like it, after the composition of it: it is holy, and it shall be holy upon you.
>
> Whosoever compoundeth any like it, or whosoever putteth any of it upon a stranger, shall be cut off from the people." Exodus 30:32-33

This was an extreme penalty for those who would use the anointing oil for a purpose other than that for which the Lord originally intended it. It was designated as holy oil. Holy speaks to separation unto God; it's for his use only not for ourselves.

> "Moses then took the anointing oil and anointed the tabernacle and all that was in it, and consecrated them." Leviticus 8:10

If God required furniture to be anointed, how much more does he require his human vessels to be anointed? **Do we highly esteem the anointing of God? Or do we see it as a commodity to be picked up and used on our way to the good life?** Very expensive ingredients, tempered finely together, were required to make it up and God commanded that it was not to be poured out on man's flesh. Furthermore, we must not concoct something that resembles it or is the equivalent of the holy anointing oil.

The ingredients or spices used were usually associated with the anointing of a body for burial. They had a very distinctive fragrance, and were not to be employed for the purposes of men, but God's only.

What we see today in general is an elevation of men's flesh and ambition, paraded as the anointing. How many can distinguish between their own human personality and the holy anointing of God?

This is so difficult because the anointing has been so devalued that it resembles something man-made. The gift of gab and public oration is seen as the anointing of God, they are able to sway a crowd and produce an emotional response. This is applauded as a move of God.

We run from seminar to seminar to catch the latest catch phrase so we can captivate our congregations of mostly shallow, materialistic Christians who have not yet grown to the reality that they are being used of men, whilst God waits in the shadows to use us for his glory. Many believe that a four year matriculation from some university or seminary, is suffering enough and they have paid a price for this anointing. God forbid! Paul and Peter cringed at the thought of a shortcut to God's most precious of entities, the anointing. We need to cry out again for fresh wind and fresh fire so we can be rescued from our current rut.

Christ The Anointed One

Throughout the ages God has often used types and shadows to speak to his people. For example as Lori Wilkes states in her ground breaking book, The Costly Anointing, "In the Old Testament the anointing always took on a three-fold nature. First, there were the anointers, such as Samuel and Elisha. Second there were the ones being anointed such as Aaron and David, and third was the anointing, seen in the holy anointing oil. The New Testament also reveals to us these threefold realities of the anointing in the God-head. First, the father is the anointer. "God anointed Jesus of Nazareth with the Holy Ghost and with power: who went about doing good and healing all who were oppressed of the devil; for God was with him." Acts 10:38. Second the son is the Anointed "He first findeth his own brother Simon, and saith unto him, we have found the Messiah, which is being interpreted, the anointed one." (John 1:41

paraphrased). Third, the Holy Spirit is the Anointing (1 John 2:20, 27). These examples of the unity of the God-head in its nature and function help us to see the administration of the anointing. Since the Lord Jesus is the Christ, the Anointed, the believers which constitute his body receive the same anointing. Christ, being the head, reigns over the members of his body (1Corinthians 12:12, 27) Christians are anointed ones, members of Christ. The Holy Spirit is that precious anointing oil that abides within all of us.

With that foundation set, let us examine the true anointing. The word "anointing" actually means "to rub" and can be interpreted as meaning "to smear with oil". This simple act takes on an eternal weight when God's instructions are followed, such as who is to be anointed and when it should happen. Outside of this it is man-made and holds no heavenly significance. The anointing then, to put it simply in our contemporary Post-Calvary dispensation, is **PUTTING ON CHRIST.**

"...which is Christ in you the hope of glory."
Col 1:27

Christ which is to say the anointed one is our anointing, and he has anointed us with the Holy Spirit. This is no light thing. To be used of God to fulfill his mandate, God has invested the complete God-head into his body, the bride of Christ.

In the gospels, John the Baptizer, declared unto us the promise: - "...he shall baptize you with the Holy Ghost and fire (Matthew 3:11). The person referred to in the text is Jesus. He is our baptizer. How can we take this for granted?

The Anointing is not a particular way of speaking; it has nothing to do with the pitch of your voice or goose-bumps on the skin of the audience. If this were true the secular quartet called The Temptations is perhaps the most anointed group in the world. We are losing all sense of God's presence in our generation and we are hewing out for ourselves our own cisterns of Godly things as seems good to us. The precious things of yesteryear are being trampled upon with great impunity and arrogance and there needs to be a halt in the slaughter. I will quickly add, that not everything that came from yesterday was good, righteous or even holy, but Jeremiah the prophet clearly states to us the first standard one should have when he declares that he is God's spokesman/woman or one who is being used of God.

> "...and thou shall stand before me: and if thou take forth the precious from the vile (profane), thou shalt become my spokesman..." Jeremiah 15:19 (Author's emphasis).

We cannot discard the old anymore because it is not relevant today, because principles are timeless. When we start to see the precious in what appears worthless and begin speaking it, we start to become the prophetic people we must be to accomplish the mandate of God for this hour.

The anointing needs to be restored to the psyche of the church, the true anointing. To further amplify the definition, the anointing is God's response to the need of a people to draw close to him. The anointing, I believe is not triggered because the preacher is present, but because there is a need present and God is the only answer to that situation and he will get the glory.

Destroyed Yokes

> "And it shall come to pass in that day, that this burden shall be taken away from off thy shoulder and his yoke from off thy neck, and the yoke shall be destroyed because of the anointing."
> Isaiah 10:27

The bible clearly teaches that the yoke is destroyed by reason of the anointing. Could it be that the reason so many desperate and fragile saints come to church hurting and leave the same way, is no true anointing present to heal them? Our amplifiers and microphones are blurring even louder now, but amidst the ear splitting screams from the pulpit there is no change occurring in the people in the pews. A quiet cry is getting louder and louder as desperate saints are now asking "Where are the miracles of our fathers?" It would seem that our best years are behind us. God forbid! I believe that our best years are just over the next horizon, where God is now preparing new breed of believers to be used by his Spirit to wrought miracles, signs and wonders that will surpass those of the Charismatic and Pentecostal revivals. Yes! Let me pause and prophesy:-

God is bringing up a generation who will stand on the shoulders of the great saints of old and declare like Elijah, a word that will affect nations. Not just churches or communities, but nations. They will be fearless, nameless, but full of integrity. They will go by the name "The Lord is their God". Great signs and wonders will accompany their lives and the world will rush in with much anger to persecute them but they will not be deterred, they will grow stronger, this will be those who will usher in the end of days. Amen.

Are we ready to be used of God? He wants to anoint you afresh right now. He wants to endue you with fresh fire; he wants to use you for his eternal purpose. There are a people whose God will be the Lord. That statement might sound out of place today, but if we scrutinize many church-goers, we would wonder "Who is their God?

I believe one of the major yokes that needs to be destroyed in this age is what I call a yoke of blindness over the minds of unbelievers.

"But if our gospel be hid, it is hid to them that are lost:

In whom the god of this world hath blinded the minds of them which believe not, lest the light of the glorious gospel of Christ, who is the image of God, should shine unto them." 2 Corinthians 4:3-4

The sad thing about this passage is that we have people who go to church every week who still don't believe in God totally. The spirit of blindness has yoked them to the world and they cannot see themselves living outside of the limitations of the world around them. They cannot comprehend the faith of men like Abraham, who would leave everything he knew to follow a God he was only acquainted with. They are unable to understand, the apostle Paul, who gave up the best life possible as a Pharisee to follow a God who he at one time relentlessly persecuted, and with only a visitation coupled with temporary blindness led him to give it all up to serve God to the death. That kind of faith is baffling to the ordinary church-goers, who neither knows God nor understands his ordinances. They have been too long yoked to the things of the world. The purpose of God has been choked out of their consciousness and is replaced by a rabid drive to achieve as much as they can in this life.

This yoke and others such as sickness, disease, mass hysteria to name a few can only be confronted by one who walks in the true anointing. Such a one will not be liked or promoted by men. He/she will be designated a rebel, an outsider, but when they speak the atmosphere around them will become distorted; principalities and demon spirits will be displaced without even being addressed by name. Why? Because a true anointing is in the city. Lord let this be me should be your prayer right now... If there is a shred of Holy Ghost desperation left within, you will put down this book and cry out for a true anointing. He did it before, he can do it again.

It is time that you were blessed and highly favored of God and it is equally true that God wants you to be truly anointed so you can be used of God to bring him glory. All types of yokes being broken, is evidence that the anointing is present. It could be in a dance, a verse of poetry, a mime, the telling of a story, even preaching the word of God, once the vessel that God is using is anointed by God for that moment every yoke situated within that sphere will be broken. The Apostles of the Book of Acts were so anointed that even their shadows were used of God to bring deliverance, pieces of clothing used by these men were used as a point of contact to wrought great healings. The olive oil was used as a point of contact to touch the afflicted and they were all healed miraculously. (It happened before, it can happen again.) We must however position ourselves as the men of old so that we can be mightily used of God. They were humble, contrite in heart, they pursued holiness and lived in the conscious fact that their Lord and Savior Jesus Christ could put in his appearance at any time. They were rapture ready, men and women of Issachar, who understood the times and knew what they should do. Yes! There is so much to learn in such a short time.

We must as servants of God, put away the worldly appetite from our bellies so we can only be satisfied by the word of God in our mouths. Jesus declared to his wary disciples who saw him ministering to the Samaritan woman

> "My meat is to do the will of him that sent me." (John4:34)

We cannot effectively wage warfare against an enemy who we depend on for daily sustenance. We must also avoid the temptation of being method driven versus seekers of an intimate relationship with Christ. Too many of our preachers are too reliant on the methods they have learnt rather than totally depending on God.

We must realize that yesterday's manna is totally useless today. We must seek the Lord for fresh bread. Jesus declared in the Lord's Prayer; give us this day our daily bread. Manna fell daily, if you are not in the know, where God's current revelation is concerned, maybe you haven't gotten out of your tent in a while, feeding on stale bread while God's fresh now word is drying up outside the door of your heart.

Blessed are those who hunger and thirst after righteousness. The blessing is in the hunger not in being filled. Get desperate for him today. Another important lesson we who desire to be used God must learn is that our enemy is wise and he will not be caught in the same way twice or with the same generational strategy, he has learnt to adapt. So we must follow the only being in the entire universe that has defeated him. In 2 Samuel 5:17-25 we see a good example of this lesson.

> "But when the Philistines heard that they had anointed David king over Israel, all the Philistines came up to seek David; and David heard *of it,* and went down to the hold.
>
> The Philistines also came and spread themselves in the valley of Rephaim.
>
> And David enquired of the LORD, saying, Shall I go up to the Philistines? wilt thou deliver them into mine hand? And the LORD said unto David, Go up: for I will doubtless deliver the Philistines into thine hand.
>
> And David came to Baalperazim, and David smote them there, and said, The LORD hath

broken forth upon mine enemies before me, as the breach of waters. Therefore he called the name of that place Baalperazim.

And there they left their images, and David and his men burned them.

And the Philistines came up yet again, and spread themselves in the valley of Rephaim.

And when David enquired of the LORD, he said, Thou shalt not go up; *but* fetch a compass behind them, and come upon them over against the mulberry trees.

And let it be, when thou hearest the sound of a going in the tops of the mulberry trees, that then thou shalt bestir thyself: for then shall the LORD go out before thee, to smite the host of the Philistines.

And David did so, as the LORD had commanded him; and smote the Philistines from Geba until thou come to Gazer."

It was the same enemy, same place, two different strategies that brought victory on both occasions. The common denominator in both scenarios however, is that David inquired of the Lord. After the first major victory at Baalperazim, he didn't just jump off into the second fight, he inquired again. This time God said "Thou shalt not go up" Godly restraint must be one of the characteristics of saints of God today. To be used of God we must wait on the move of the Spirit before we move. God told David wait for the sound in the top of the mulberry trees and this time I will break forth upon your enemies. In the previous battle David broke forth on the Philistines and defeated them. They must have prepared for David and his men the second time around, but this time David attacked from the rear and a supernatural being attacked from the front, God.

How many battles have we lost because we rush head first into it, losing our heads in the process? Those who are truly anointed and used of God have learnt how to wait before the Lord. The world today is making us agitated, and anxious; everything is fast, fast food, fast money, express lanes at the banks or supermarkets, fast lanes on the highway. We are used to getting everything fast. The world is training us well – to miss God.

Reclaim control of your life, many of the things, that you deem must be done right now, really can wait until after five minutes of prayer. We have discarded the important things of God for the urgent things of this life. The true anointing is demanding a re-prioritizing of our lives. Start today, ask the Holy Spirit to help you and see how your life becomes more meaningful.

Become Another Man

The Bible records a truly fascinating story in 1 Samuel10:1-8 we see where God through Samuel anointed Saul to become Israel's first king. King Saul did many evil things as a king; however we will not focus on any of these. There was a moment in his life that the anointing changed him and caused him to be a sign and a wonder before all of Israel. You see, even though God was displeased with their request for a King at that time, he still validated Saul's leadership by bestowing upon Saul the spirit of prophecy. (For further context, it was Moses who declared that God would raise up a leader like himself- speaking of Messiah) The Bible teaches us in verse 6 of chapter 10,

> "And the Spirit of the Lord will come upon thee and thou shalt prophesy with them and shalt be turned into another man."

King Saul prophesied like the prophets that day, he was not called to the prophetic ministry he was just anointed by God. I believe one of the telltale signs of an anointed saint of God is the spirit of prophecy operating in their lives. You could be a bank teller, or a bus driver, if you are anointed by God the spirit of prophecy would be evident. The anointing turned Saul into another man, so much so that it disturbed the status quo of the then backslidden nation. Questions were being asked like

'Who is his father?' Apparently you had to be born in the right family to be a prophet. In one move God destroyed the mindsets and caused men to think outside of their boxes.

Just like Saul, God is seeking a people in whom he can place his anointing and truly turn them into vessels of change.

Joel 2:28

"And it shall come to pass afterwards that I will pour out my spirit upon all flesh, and your sons and daughters shall prophesy…"

This promise is being fulfilled even today, it started on the day of Pentecost in the upper room and the spirit hasn't ceased being poured out on men. What is scarce are true vessels upon which the true anointing needs to be poured; as you consider your ways today remember, we live in a time of AIDS, financial uncertainty, global disasters, hysteria, depression and hopelessness is at its highest level in all of human history. We need something fresh from heaven as nothing earthly has the power to change our situations. As many of the most sought after and entertaining churches of the nineties are closed out and have become relics of the past. Only a fresh anointing from God can break this cycle of darkness which has captivated the world. Jesus the anointed one stands ready to anoint- Are you willing to be

CLAY IN THE MASTER'S HAND

"The word which came to Jeremiah from the LORD, saying,

Arise, and go down to the potter's house, and there I will cause thee to hear my words.

Then I went down to the potter's house, and, behold, he wrought a work on the wheels.

And the vessel that he made of clay was marred in the hand of the potter: so he made it again another vessel, as seemed good to the potter to make *it.*" Jeremiah 18:1-4

Mankind over the eons of time has developed an over exaggerated view of himself. We as created beings live in extremes. We either have a lesser view which leads to low self esteem and other toxic self defeating attitudes, or we see ourselves as gods in charge of our own destiny, we put ourselves at the centre of the universe. In fact, at one time, not many years ago this philosophy was the most dominant thought there was and we know how wrong that was.

We are in need of balance, **as how we see ourselves is critical to how we relate to our creator.** When Adam saw his sinful self without any hope of redemption, he hid from his Creator among the trees. Since then sadly enough we are still hiding among the trees. Our only hope of realizing our true identity must come from the mind of the one who created us. How he sees us must form the foundation of how we will start seeing ourselves. Somewhere between the two extremes mentioned earlier is a middle perspective of ourselves that we must come to know so that we can become who we were created to be.

The Potters Touch

God instructed Jeremiah to go down to the potter's house to see what he was doing so that he (Jeremiah) could hear the word of the Lord. I believe the Lord is calling this generation see his word being performed as they hear it spoken. We are not just excited by the sermonizing of scriptures we want to see the word be performed as the Apostle Paul taught the church at Thessalonica. God wanted to reveal to Jeremiah his heart towards his people Israel during that time, but the lessons and principles are still relevant to us in our modern day.

Having never done any pottery work before, I too felt the need to observe a potter at work: thanks to the internet I did not have to leave home (one point for modern technology☺). I saw a work of great skill, patience, imagination and love. The potter I observed seemed to have a love for the clay. He treated it with much care; it was scrutinized, molded by hand over and over again, it was processed with water so it would become flexible in his hands. It was stretched out, rolled out, being constantly touched by the potter and only after it was deemed worthy to be <u>used</u>, and then it was put on the potter's wheel.

After observing this careful preparation by mere potters, Jeremiah chapter eighteen and verse four struck me differently. The Bible teaches,

> "And the vessel that he made of clay was marred in the hand if the potter..."

The Strong's Exhaustive Concordance of the Bible renders the word marred to mean, devastate, to ruin, to decay; other meaning include to injure, to be corrupted.[v]

I wondered if the problem was with the potter's lack of experience or if the clay was just bad. Why should a scripture that seems so unassuming cause me days of perplexity; but it did. Then a thought came to me, what if the potter knew all along that the clay was defective, yet he still brought it to usefulness. Instead of casting it out, he worked with its imperfections and produced a work that was pleasing to him. The Complete Jewish Bible Translation by David H. Stern put it this way:-

> "Whenever a pot he made came out imperfect, the potter took the clay and made another pot with it, in whatever shape suited him." (Jeremiah 18:4 CJB)

Our imperfections are not a deterrent to God's plan in our lives. He took the same clay and made another pot with it, as it seemed good to him. As I write this the great hymn writer comes to mind. Fanny Crosby; blind from infancy through a medical mishap and destined by the world's standards to live a life of obscurity and rejection, as she would have been severely handicapped by her blindness. She may have been relegated to touch only a certain group of persons, never to be heard from or seen. I could put myself in her parent's shoes, who must have had so many hopes and plans for their lovely healthy child; they would not have been prepared for the trauma. Never to enjoy the sunrise or sunset again, never again they thought would she be normal. Fanny Crosby, proved to be anything but normal, she in her blindness, I believe, had a clearer vision of her Lord than many of us sighted saints. Let us for a moment examine this seemingly marred clay and how she was so powerfully used of God, to touch her generation. Presidents, First Ladies; how her words sparked revivals and how a nation's consciousness was affected by one who did not have earthly vision but who had heavenly insight.

Fanny Crosby

Born Frances Jane Crosby (March 24, 1820 – February 12, 1915), she was a Methodist rescue missions worker, poet, lyricist, composer and lobbyist. She wrote over 8000 hymns, with over 100 million copies of her songs printed. At six weeks old Crosby caught a cold and developed inflammation of the eyes. Mustard poultices were applied to treat the discharges. According to Crosby, the procedure damaged her optic nerves and blinded her. Her Father died the year she was born, so she was raised by her mother and maternal grandmother. These women grounded Crosby in Protestant Christian Principles, helping her, for example, to memorize long passages from the Bible.

At the age of eight Crosby wrote her first poem which described her condition. Crosby later remarked, "It seems intended by the blessed providence of God that I should be blind and I thank him for the dispensation. If prefect earthly sight were offered me tomorrow I would not accept it. I might not have sung hymns to the praise of God if I had been distracted by the beautiful and interesting things about me."[vi]

Such devotion to God seems devilish today; she was thanking God for her impediment, even praising God for it. Considering that without it life might not have the joy or meaning it currently held. She was able to find peace with God and herself and live a life truly as a champion. I am not saying for one minute that we should take all sickness or evil as from our loving father, no way! Everything in our lives that is ungodly or evil should be resisted and contended against. Even Ms. Crosby fought her blindness; she went to the top surgeons of her time to seek a remedy for her ailment.

Similarly, I know several persons of good fortune who are being used of God even though they are wealthy, in health and in great standing in their communities. We will highlight some later. However, the enemy has robbed so many of us of the privilege of being used of God because we consider that our imperfections are a hindrance. Moses was a stutterer, he had a speech impediment but God called him to confront a King and he was to speak forth the word of God. God knows we are imperfect, so he empowers us by making us another vessel.

Graced To Be

"And lest I should be exalted above measure through the abundance of the revelations, there was given to me a thorn in the flesh, the messenger of Satan to buffet me, lest I should be exalted above measure.

For this thing I besought the Lord thrice, that it might depart from me.

And he said unto me, my grace is sufficient for thee: for my strength is made perfect in weakness. Most gladly therefore will I rather glory in my infirmities, that the power of Christ may rest upon me." 2 Corinthians 12:7-9

There is a major difference, I believe, between weakness as identified by the Apostle Paul versus sinfulness as a weakness of the flesh in the believer. God's response to man's weakness is his grace. The grace of God is the thing that enables us to do the things of God that we would not necessarily be able to do. It shows up as God's favor which is not just a title but an active force that God employs for his children to bring them into his purpose. The grace of God is not released to cover over our sin so we can sin continually. Paul answers this question in Romans 6:2 "God forbid. How shall we that are dead to sin, live any longer therein?"

The question of God's grace in a believer's life is one of submission. Have we yielded all our members to the work of the Holy Spirit? If the answer is yes, then in those areas where we are unable to fulfill God's mandate through our own efforts, he empowers us. He releases grace sufficient enough to make us perfect in that area. Paul refers to his infirmities, or his imperfections, just like Ms. Crosby's blindness, which had the potential to stop the flow of God through her.

By employing all kinds of self defeating mechanisms such as self pity, fear of rejection, fear of man, low self esteem, low self concept, the list goes on. She could have remained handicapped by her blindness, but she instead rested on Jesus. It fueled her love for him even more. The Apostle aptly put it thus,

"Most gladly therefore will rather glory in my infirmities, that the power of Christ may <u>rest</u> upon me." 2Corinthians 12:9b

This is crazy talk in our modern culture of physics, astronauts and Ivy League Universities. The Apostle was praising God for his infirmities because in his mind, the more infirmities he encountered personally, the more Christ would rest upon him. That was his reason for living – Christ and him crucified. He wanted more of Christ; Paul wanted to see how far he could go in Christ and still remain a citizen of this earth. However, many saints today want to live as close to the world and its beauty and see if they can still remain citizens of heaven. Our Theology takes us too often too close to the brink of backsliding, not totally submerged into the spirit of God. Those who dare to walk as Paul or even Fanny Crosby are cautioned to seek wisdom, as we would not be relevant to the world. I beg to differ; I believe only a soul totally immersed in the spirit of God can be of value in this world.

The enemy is trying to devalue us in this world by devaluing the importance of the heavenly perspective. Listen to what this great warrior of the faith said, "When I get to heaven, the first face that shall ever gladden my sight will be that of my savior." When asked about her blindness, Crosby was reported as saying that, "had it not been for her affliction she might not have had so good an education, or so great an influence and certainly not so fine a memory"[vii]

She along with all of us saints we are graced by God to be everything he has planned for us – clay, even if it means he will have to keep making us over and over again, until we become good in his sight. The clay has no power over itself; it is molded into what the potter designed in his heart. The clays beauty and usefulness is in the Potter's mind. Jeremiah 29:11 states

> "For I know the thoughts I think towards you, said, the Lord, thoughts of peace, and not of evil, to give you an expected end."

> Wow! To be in the hand of a Potter who thinks beautiful thoughts – yes we are!

> "And the Lord God formed man of the dust of the ground and breathed into his nostrils the breath of life and man became a living soul. "Genesis 2:7

The creation of Adam was so intimate. God formed man this suggests that God interacted with the clay he formed just like a potter forms a clay pot. Every contour was examined and thought out, our legs, eyelashes; he touched man's face and smoothed out the rough edges, just like a potter. Then he came even closer and blew breath into our nostrils, and man became a living soul- when his eyes were open for the first time, the very first face he saw was God. What would men give up today for just one glimpse of eternity. Everything

We have become ugly and useless to God because the clay has decided to form itself. We reject him every time we go our own way. The potter is the only one who can validate the clay and make it something useful, because whatever he calls it that's what it is. I remember going to a craft market once and I saw a strange looking clay jar, I inquired about it and I was told it was a masterpiece. It was more valuable than all the other pieces of work on show, I looked around and thought there were other pieces of pottery there that were more beautiful in my eyes but, that did not affect the potter nor the value of his prized masterpiece. You see the value was not set by the buyer but by the Creator. I learned a lesson that day, that the thoughts of the Creator are more important than just us window shoppers. Even with our imperfections God still claims we are fearfully and wonderfully made, set apart for his glory in the earth.

As we conclude with Fanny, it was reported that she would write six to seven hymns per day. She stated that she would never pen a poem or hymn without first praying for inspiration. She is known for great hymns such as, Blessed Assurance, Pass me not oh Gentle Savior, Praise Him Praise Him, Rescue the Perishing and the great, To God be the Glory. Towards the end of her life she totally dedicated herself to the poor, even though she was well known as a hymn writer, she considered herself a friend of the poor. She was one of the first women to address the United States Senate. She lobbied all over the eastern United States for the rights of the blind to receive an equal education. Her work in the slums of New York was what she wanted to define her. She is not known for her preaching but many souls were saved during her years of preaching at the city mission and at the YMCA in New York. Though her hymn writing declined in later years, Crosby was active in speaking engagements and missionary work among America's urban poor almost until she died. Her hymns are still as powerful today as they were over fifty years ago.

Generations will know your work when you are used of God. There is a people on the earth who will be known as the people of God, not only the Jews but Christians who have surrendered to the hand of the potter and have become something beautiful which the world cannot corrupt but only marvel at. Such were the apostles, such were the saints of old and so shall we be also.

THE FEAR OF GOD; THE DEFINING CHARACTERISTIC

"The fear of the Lord is to hate evil; pride and arrogance and the evil way, and the perverted mouth I hate." (Proverbs 8:13 NAS)

The fear of God is one of the most important defining characteristics of the life of a true believer. He or she exemplifies a healthy respect and love for the presence and person of God. When we study the lives of the old patriarchs we see how they truly revered the Lord and this translated them to a place in God's service that is still the standard today.

The issue of fear is of critical importance as we go on our life's journey with Christ, because fear has within it the power to determine our destiny. On whosoever we place our fear will either derail us or establish God's purpose on the earth. Even though fear is understood by most psychologists as an emotional feeling that is produced when one feels threatened or overwhelmed, the Bible teaches us differently about fear. It is almost as if the Bible writers got more serious when the topic of fear was introduced.

For over thirty years the world was gripped in fear. It was called the Cold war. The fear of a nuclear strike from either superpower, the Soviet Union or the United States, kept the world on edge. The fear of such a war was so debilitating that if there was news of any nuclear movement by either side the other would be on high alert, closing down shops, schools and offices, children would do gas mask drills. Soldiers would return to barracks, war time strategies would be implemented all because someone moved a missile. Fear used in the wrong way can lead to chaos, anarchy and even death. This I believe the devil knows, so fear is one of his major weapons against the saints.

The Bible however teaches,

> "By the fear of the Lord one keeps away from evil". (Proverbs 29:25 NAS) Further more it teaches

> "The fear of the Lord is the beginning of wisdom: and the knowledge of the holy is understanding." Proverbs 9:10

If we truly fear the Lord we will not fear anyone else. The Apostle Paul reasoned,

> "If I were still trying to please men I would not be a bondservant of Christ." Galatians 10:1.

To honor and respect the Lord is to be set free from all fear. As we investigate the issue of fear we must come to understand that the product of fear is not the only issue,

I believe the external or internal stimuli that produces fear must be ventilated as we examine the topic, because I don't believe God wants to use fear to threaten us to serve him. In fact, he stated in 2 Timothy1:7

> "For God hath not given us the spirit of fear, but or power and of love and of a sound mind."

So obviously there are two different kinds of fear presented here. I would categorize them as the fear of the Lord versus the fear of the enemy, or the clash of two wisdoms.

Wisdom is loosely defined as the use of knowledge. The Knowledge of God is meant to draw us closer to Him in reverential holiness. It is to show us God's unfailing love, and desire for us that should produce in us the desire to change our ways and follow after him. That's what the fear of the Lord was created to produce – sons of God.

The fear of the devil leads us away from God and into self. The fear of the devil is wrapped up in the fear of death; hence the definition of the fear of harm is construed. God doesn't want us to run to him only because we fear harm, he wants us to run to him because we love him. Paul continued to exhort us,

> "For ye have not received the spirit of bondage again to fear; but ye have received the spirit of adoption whereby we cry Abba, Father."
> Romans 8:15

The work of the cross was not only to redeem us to God but also to destroy the ultimate weapon of the enemy, fear. We are no longer governed by this negative emotion, we are free to be his sons, and we can call him father, without any fear of harm or retribution. As we further break down this topic, however, I want to now zero in on the real issue; that I believe can adversely affect our being used of God. I strongly believe that many believers are overcome by this subtle spirit. I think it forms the early stages of a minister's or ministry's downfall, a weapon from hell itself – it is called the fear of man.

Fear Of Man

"The fear of man brings a snare" (Proverbs 29:25 NAS).

The pressure to please people is as deadly as cancer in the body. The pressure of what people were saying caused Moses to use his rod in a manner the Lord had not stated. The greatest of all the patriarchs was defeated, not because of a demonic attack, but by the weariness brought about by the people. Many a ministry has fallen by the sword of fear of man.

To be justified in the sight of your peers or to be viewed as a success from the world's perspective is opposite to the view held by God. In fact it is utterly detestable in the sight of God if we esteem or elevate man above God. Jesus rebuked the Pharisees and declared,

> "Ye are they which justify yourself before men but God knoweth your hearts, for that which is highly esteemed among men is abomination in the sight of God." Luke 16:15

It is easy to discern when one fears the devil or even death; however it's very difficult to see when the fear of man is at work. The one under the influence can easily justify his or her actions. There might even be a touch of good-will involved, but it is diabolic. To be used of God is to be delivered from the applause of men. It must be seen for what it is – dung. If we are compelled to seek the esteem of men, we will be found doing that which is abominable. Jesus put this in the same category as idolatry, bestiality and doing the most detestable of things. We must break free of what men think of us and solely rely on what God says. We must determine who we are going to serve man or God. We cannot do both.

Jesus in his earthly walk desired only to please his Father, no matter what controversy it caused, the fall out of disciples or support, he stayed true to the worship of the Father. "Everything he did was for the purpose of the Father without regard to Himself, even though it resulted in His own suffering and death. God is waiting for the corporate church to make exactly the same demonstration in order that the age might conclude."[viii]

We are at war, with the devil, the world and our carnal flesh; there is no relenting, no respite, the attacks are continual and without mercy; we must determine in our hearts to follow Christ alone. The pressure to fit into this world and its system, that is to be culturally accepted is enormous, just ask any teenager. The way the world is constituted is not just by happenstance. There is a method behind the seeming madness. We are pushed to conform to this world and its standards in everything. The way we dress, the way we eat, everything is competing for our attention. We must, however learn to focus ourselves on the things which really matter eternally.

The approval of man will lead us into a snare, a snare is a trap used to catch prey. Many times the prey is unaware of the predicament it has been lured into by following an appetizing meal. To be operating in the fear of man might seem to be initially less dangerous than the other things such as adultery, idolatry, lying and so on, but, this is a trap! To be constantly seeking the esteem of men would put us at enmity with God, simply because His ways are not or ways and His thoughts are not ours. As mentioned before in the gospel of Luke16:15

"What is highly esteemed by men is detestable in the sight of God."

<u>Satanic Strategy</u>

There is an incident in the gospel that is worth serious consideration at this point. In the book of Matthew chapter 16 verse23- Jesus said unto Peter,

> "Get thee behind me, Satan: thou art an offense unto me: for thou savourest not the things that be of God, but those that be of men."

Jesus called his top picked disciple, Satan, or adversary, deceiver equating him to a murderer. A closer look at the full scenario from verse twenty-one might puzzle the casual Bible reader, as they try to understand Jesus' response to Peter's actions.

> "From that time forth began Jesus to shew unto his disciples, how that he must go unto Jerusalem, and suffer many things of the elders and chief priests and scribes, and be killed, and be raised again the third day.
>
> Then Peter took him, and began to rebuke him, saying, Be it far from thee, Lord: this shall not be unto thee. Matthew16:22-23

Peter did what any man would do, if he felt that his best friend was talking nonsense. Be it far from you… this cannot happen, you are the Lord. On the surface it looks quite innocent, however Jesus' reply reveals a deeper motive that was not expressed, but was the foundation or root of Peter's rebuke. Jesus was their leader, he was also their source, and everything they had come into during that three year period was because of Jesus. His death would prove catastrophic to them, not only spiritually or emotionally but also materially. Further on in the gospel of Matthew, Peter's response to Jesus during the discourse with the rich young ruler is instructive,

"Then answered Peter and said unto him, Behold, we have forsaken all, and followed thee; what shall we have therefore?

And Jesus said unto them, Verily I say unto you, That ye which have followed me, in the regeneration when the Son of man shall sit in the throne of his glory, ye also shall sit upon twelve thrones, judging the twelve tribes of Israel.

And every one that hath forsaken houses, or brethren, or sisters, or father, or mother, or wife, or children, or lands, for my name's sake, shall receive an hundredfold, and shall inherit everlasting life.

But many *that are* first shall be last; and the last *shall be* first." Matthew 19:27-30

You could clearly see the legitimate concern by Peter, we have forsaken all to follow you; what shall we have? Peter was putting forward the point that they deserved something; Do you see Jesus how good we have been? Peter's rebuke of Jesus was motivated by self, because it sought to protect its self interest. The purpose of the Father was dismissed out of hand in comparison to the purpose of Peter's survival. In this Jesus called his friend satanic. Peter was not foaming at the mouth, speaking in another voice or squirming on his belly like a serpent. Most of our ideas of what is satanic fall far below what God calls satanic. It is around us every day, it is everywhere but we do not recognize it, because we have an image of The Exorcist in our heads of how a demon possessed person should behave. I can assure you that this image of what satanic activity looks like came directly from hell to deceive the saints.

There are satanic activities in the Church, in our families, every time there is rebellion, there is Satan. Every time someone is derailed from fulfilling God's purpose in their lives, it's satanic. The Apostle John declared:-

> "Little children, it is the last time: and as ye have heard that antichrist shall come, even now are there many antichrists; whereby we know that it is the last time." 1 John 2:18

Peter was more concerned about Jesus being unharmed over the will of God and he was called Satan. To be used of God we must understand and be able to communicate the call of God for our lives. We are not a product of our society; we have been born again from above, sent with a holy calling to do damage to the kingdom of darkness. We are not an ordinary people; hence we cannot continue to live like mere men, subject to the condition of our circumstances. We are believers of Christ, walking out a destiny that was given to us from our father and nothing should be able to rob us of seeing our mission a success in the eyes of God. John went on to teach us,

> "Love not the world neither the things that are
> in the world. If any man love the world, the love
> of the father is not in him."1 John 2:15

The world wants us to be afraid of God, just like Adam after he sinned and hid from the presence of his creator. Man has been hiding ever since, but now in Christ we can cry boldly Abba, Father and reverentially fear God. Break the snare today, decide in your heart that only what God says will matter and walk out your new found faith and see victory in every battle.

David And Saul

We couldn't end our Chapter without referring to one of the greatest contrasts between fear of God and fear of man recorded in the Bible. I believe the greatest difference between these Kings was in who they wanted to please. King Saul feared the people more than he feared the Lord, whilst David feared the Lord more than the people.

King Saul constantly went against the purposes of God because he highly esteemed the love of the people above his service to God (1 Samuel13:11)

> "And Samuel said, What hast thou done? And Saul said, Because I saw that the people were scattered from me, and *that* thou camest not within the days appointed, and *that* the Philistines gathered themselves together at Michmash;

When Saul was commanded to wait until the prophet Samuel returned to make a sacrifice to the Lord before going into battle, he could not wait because he saw the people scattering from him. As Rick Joyner puts it, "Anyone that has walked in leadership in the body of Christ understands the pressure which caused Saul to stumble. When the people begin to scatter and the enemy advances at the same time, the compulsion to do something is very great, even when the Lord has commanded us to wait."[ix]

To keep the people united was a noble cause, yet it went against God's command to wait on Samuel. He went and illegally performed a priestly act that was not permitted for him, because he would have looked in the eyes of the people. To give in to those pressures is to risk the anointing. I contrast when David came under the same people pressure at Ziklag,

> "And David was greatly distressed; for the people spake of stoning him, because the soul of all the people was grieved, every man for his sons and for his daughters: but David encouraged himself in the LORD his God.
>
> And David said to Abiathar the priest, Ahimelech's son, I pray thee, bring me hither the ephod. And Abiathar brought thither the ephod to David.
>
> And David enquired at the LORD, saying, Shall I pursue after this troop? shall I overtake them? And he answered him, Pursue: for thou shalt surely overtake *them,* and without fail recover *all.*" 1 Samuel 30:6-8

I cannot imagine the pressure David must have endured that day. His faithful army was turning against him because of their great distress. They had lost their homes, families and all reason for living. David himself had his two wives taken captive. The natural thing to do was to retaliate, it's only human. We are taught to lash out when backed into a corner.

The Bible however declares something that defines David's character, amidst all his short comings and failures, David feared the Lord more than he feared men and their opinions. The Bible said he, encouraged himself in the Lord his God. What strength, it almost seems other worldly. In his moment of great distress, he made time to humble himself before the Lord. Whilst King Saul was quick to act to protect his self interest, David waited before the Lord even under threat of stoning from his own men. He wasn't pressured into action because it seemed "gospel like", the right thing to do, he waited until the Lord gave him clear instructions. If we are to function in true spiritual leadership, we must be in submission to God alone.

David's prayer before the Lord was even more startling. He inquired of the Lord if he should pursue his enemies or not. What? His wives were kidnapped; he did not know what kind of harm's way they were in. Quick action was required; to pursue the enemy was the clear and obvious choice. It wasn't rocket science, there seemed no need to seek God about something so obvious, but David sought the Lord anyway. He knew that victory or failure hinged on him knowing God's will rather than responding to the threats of his men.

David's life is still speaking to us today; we must develop a strong and healthy fear of God before we can be effectively used of God in this generation. Many of the tenets of Gospel truths are being discarded today as being out of touch with our modern way of thinking and living. Many Christians are living in compromise today as the world devalues our Christian ideals and relegates them to draconian, unrealistic rules that should be abandoned and rejected. True Christians are viewed as intolerant, insensitive and out of touch beings who don't have any place in this new world.

I beg to differ, we belong here and we must stand up in the face of their threats and declare like Peter before the Sanhedrin,

> "For we cannot but speak the things which we have seen and heard" Acts 4:20

Peter and the other Apostle's lives were threatened, but with boldness they defied their oppressors and continued to publicly declare the gospel. It took all that then and I believe it will take that kind of fear of God now to overcome the impending threats.

When David became King, he purposefully brought back the Ark of the Covenant to Jerusalem, the Bible declares,

> "So David danced before the Lord with all his might; and David was girded with a linen ephod." 2 Samuel 6:14

David delighted to see the presence of the Lord return to the place that God sanctified; but not everyone was so delighted.

"So David and all the house of Israel brought up the ark of the LORD with shouting, and with the sound of the trumpet.

And as the ark of the LORD came into the city of David, Michal Saul's daughter looked through a window, and saw King David leaping and dancing before the LORD; and she despised him in her heart." 2 Samuel 6:15-16

There must have been a type of protocol established that governed how the King was to behave before his subjects. Michal describes his actions as shamelessly uncovering himself before his servants and handmaids. She went further to call him a vain fellow. We know her loyalty was not to her husband, but that aside she grew up in the house of a King. How the King appears before his people is important, I wonder if she learnt that from father Saul. David was different however; his response reveals his heart,

"And David said unto Michal, *It was* before the LORD, which chose me before thy father, and before all his house, to appoint me ruler over the people of the LORD, over Israel: therefore will I play before the LORD.

And I will yet be more vile than thus, and will be base in mine own sight: and of the maidservants which thou hast spoken of, of them shall I be had in honour. 2 Samuel 6:21-22

David knew where his appointment came from, who he was accountable to, and who he should fear. His priorities were in the right order. God has a people in the earth who only have eyes for him, whose ears only have time to hear his voice; these are they who will turn the earth right side up. Proverbs teaches us, the fear of the Lord is to hate evil. To truly walk free from the bondage of sin is to truly fear the Lord. The fear of the Lord also keeps one away from evil, Proverbs 16:6. To understand this we must consider the return of one used of God to save an entire nation; Joseph.

When confronted in private with the lure and lust of Potiphar's wife he dispels her seduction by asserting,

> "...how can I do this great wickedness and sin against God." Genesis 39:9

Many do not sin because of the fear of being caught and publicly exposed- what if you were guaranteed that you would not get caught, would you still remain righteous?

Joseph, I believe was in this situation; despised by his brothers, left for dead, sold into slavery; doing the best he could to serve Potiphar his master, trying to survive. I believe he must have wondered where the God of his father was. He had heard many stories of great deliverance and provision. It must have felt like God had abandoned him. But despite all the evidence stacked against Joseph, he still feared God more than he feared for his life. There was no evidence that God was communing with him during this time. He believed God based on past history. We struggle today to fear God if we miss a rent payment or if one of our utilities is disconnected.

Joseph had a hall pass to sin. Potiphar's wife would not have said anything, he would be in a good position to maybe become free sooner than later, but he chose to reverence his God and face the consequences. His humility before God prepared him to lead the nation, Egypt and save his family, Israel. Many years in a Egyptian prison was God's training ground to form a man who was described as the Pharaoh as "Zaphnath Paaneah" which in the Coptic signifies – a revealer of secrets or the man to whom secrets are revealed; or another translation reads "the one who sees and hears from God.

It was the vicious act of his brothers that placed him in Egypt, but it was Joseph's act of holiness and fear of God that positioned him before the King and ultimately put him in the seat of leadership. We cannot live in compromise; it will rob you of your future in God. Compromise is a deadly enemy because it is so easily justified in our minds. When Saul was commanded to attack and utterly destroy the Amalikites, he attacked them and destroyed most of them; but he kept alive the king and some of the best livestock. He justified keeping the animals by saying he would offer them to the Lord. This compromise cost Saul the throne, effectively wiping away his future and even his family's future was devastated because he did not fear God.

Our actions might not seem to have immediate consequences, so we are lulled into a false sense of security, but we must aggressively go after this spirit in our lives on a daily basis, so that we will have a future.

End Time Jewels

"Then they that feared the LORD spake often one to another: and the LORD hearkened, and heard *it,* and a book of remembrance was written before him for them that feared the LORD, and that thought upon his name.

And they shall be mine, saith the LORD of hosts, in that day when I make up my jewels; and I will spare them, as a man spareth his own son that serveth him.

Then shall ye return, and discern between the righteous and the wicked, between him that serveth God and him that serveth him not." Malachi 3:16-18

The fear of the Lord as a defining characteristic has to be cultivated in the life of the believer. "Christ-like-ness" must be developed in the life of the believer. Through careful studies, much prayer and consecration, the believer will develop the character of Christ. However with the prevalence of another type of gospel, which is so popular today, that seems to downplay holiness and being sold out, we are in danger of becoming something lesser than what God requires.

The Bible teaches that there is a book that is recording the conversations of those saints that fear the Lord; and those that thought upon his name. Too little is being preached on this topic; in an attempt to not scare away the Christian with a strong message on the fear of the Lord we are inadvertently driving the presence of the Lord away from the Church with our limp-noodle sermons. So important is the topic that the Bible declares in verse 18 "and they shall be mine saith the Lord of Hosts"

Every Christian who has ever contemplated being separated from God and wondering if they would ever make it into paradise, must study this chapter in Malachi. The Lord said emphatically, and they shall be mine. He shows supreme ownership, protection and love. He went further to say,

> "In that day when I make up my jewels and I will spare them as a man spareth his own son that serveth him." Malachi 3:17

The Lord sees them as jewels, those that fear him. He will spare them as a man spareth his own son. Wow! Even before the coming of Jesus, the Father outlined to us the process of salvation. He will spare those who fear his name. They are the end-time saints, those who fear God more than they fear men, those who would put the glory of God above their very needs. These are the ones he calls his jewels.

There are so many false teacher today, showing off many lying signs and wonders. It seems so hard at times to discern between the righteous and the wicked, between those that serve the Lord and those that do not serve him. It appears that the authentic Christian is in the minority many sincere sheep are being led astray by snake oil preachers. But how can we differentiate?

When I was younger, I worked at a bank in my country, one week I was sent to a seminar on currency management. In this one week seminar the main emphasis was on dealing with counterfeit notes versus genuine. So for four days we handled and interacted with the genuine currencies. On the final day when we were doing our exit exam, the counterfeit notes were placed among the genuine. Every person in the seminar passed. We were able to easily recognize the false notes because we spent all week interacting with the real thing. What am I saying here; in order to be truly able to discern between the things of God versus the devil, we should not spend all of our time studying the devil; we must study and interact with the genuine article. We must spend most of our waking moments in the presence of God and only then we have any hope of recognizing the wolves in sheep clothing. Discernment can only happen after we have received knowledge.

Those who have been used of God have always been known for their fear of God. Abraham, Moses, King David, Deborah, Peter, Paul and so many others. It was required then and it surely is required now. God's end time army only has eyes for him, they will be ridiculed, and even persecuted, but they will be smitten by the loveliness of their Lord and just like Stephen when he was being martyred, his eyes were fixed on the prize.

There was a race to be run; there is a peculiar life to be lived, because there are crowns to be had. Until this becomes your joy, your focus, you will not be able to survive the upcoming tribulation; you will not be effectively used of God. Let us encourage ourselves in the Lord, like King David and let us pledge to seek his face, until he shows up and changes us.

CONCLUSION

TOMORROW MATTERS

"A seed shall serve him; it shall be accounted to the Lord for a generation.

They shall come, and shall declare his righteousness unto a people that shall be born, that he hath done this." Psalm 22:30-31

As I stand at the crest of this generation's wave, as we move at a swift pace into the future, my spirit is very troubled as a young man, minister and father of four beautiful children. I am concerned because of what I am seeing; it's almost like a proverb; where a changing of the guard is happening, not only in natural but in the spiritual realm. Younger, brighter more energetic leaders are taking over the reign of leadership in our nations and in the Church. The old standard bearers are passing, many are in their twilight years, and many have just simply been forgotten. This, however, is a natural part of life, the old is replaced with the new, the former is set aside for the latter; this is normal. However, my grave concern has to do with the way the <u>transition</u> is taking place.

The up and coming generation is seemingly disregarding their history. Pouring cold water on their spiritual father's and mother's fire. The past is being shoved to the back without any regard for its importance, its lessons and wisdom. The generation is summed up in a popular song "I'll do it my way!" we can go further to say we are a Burger King people that declare "have it your way". However,

> "There is a way that seemeth right to a man,
> but the end thereof are the ways of death."
> Proverbs14:12

To disregard our history is in effect to disregard God. To place no value on the experience of those who went before us is in effect devaluing ourselves. Those who were used of God before us have set the pace for us today, their story must be told, and their successes, why some failed and what the Lord did. All this is important. Contemporary thought reminds us that those who forget their history are doomed to repeat it. A great spiritual darkness looms as we venture out into our future without the wisdom or blessing of our forefathers, the danger lies in the fact that we will become a people who would do things in a way that only seems right to us. Not unlike farmers who plant crops on a field and they were never taught to let the soil rest, so after a while the yield becomes less and less until the soil becomes impotent; powerless to produce. Similarly, many fishermen are fishing the seas to extinction, while many loggers are destroying acres of forest without the wisdom of replanting. They are only governed by their needs, what is immediate. For generations farmers, fisher folk and tree cutters have been preserving their environment that they worked, however today there is a crisis as the farmers, fisher folk and many loggers are more driven by market needs, pushed to supply the demands so they can make more money, rather than considering the preservation of resources. The disregard of our past is now adversely affecting our children's future. The same is true spiritually.

Historical Context

> "And also all that generation were gathered unto their fathers: and there arose another generation after them, which knew not the LORD, nor yet the works which he had done for Israel."
> Judges 2:10

The book of Judges shares with us the deadly cycle one can come into when the ways of the Lord are rejected. Israel went into a cycle of blessings, rejecting God, enslavement to their ungodly neighbors, repentance then deliverance. This cycle continued all the way through Judges. The above mentioned passage is very revealing as we can draw a couple very important conclusions from it. Firstly, when the preceding generation passed the next generation went into apostasy. It gave two very significant reasons why. It states, "...and there arose another generation after them, which knew not the

Lord," and secondly "nor yet the works which he had done <u>for</u> Israel".

It appears that the problem was that the people just forgot about God. The Bible declares, the generation arose who did not know the Lord. The knowledge of God was not communicated to the next generation. In order that this would not happen, God had initiated a plan through Moses, in the book of Deuteronomy chapter 6, He teaches,

"And these words, which I command thee this day, shall be in thine heart:

And thou shalt teach them diligently unto thy children, and shalt talk of them when thou sittest in thine house, and when thou walkest by the way, and when thou liest down, and when thou risest up.

And thou shalt bind them for a sign upon thine hand, and they shall be as frontlets between thine eyes.

And thou shalt write them upon the posts of thy house, and on thy gates." Deuteronomy 6:6-9

God instituted a system of continually putting the knowledge of the Lord before the people. Every sphere was covered. The home, the place of work, their walking, laying down even when they rose up his words should be mentioned. This sort of word saturation was necessary, because the people did not know the Lord. They were slaves and children of slaves, living in a culture that was the antithesis of everything that God was. However, this was not done, so after the generation of Joshua and Caleb the people went a whoring after other gods. There is another reason why Israel ended up in slavery; not only because of the failure of the older generation to pass on the knowledge of God and his acts to their children, which is also evident today, but there is a second reason. I believe this reason is more apt for us today because back in Israel's history they relied upon oral tradition to know the ways of God. We all know how ineffective this can be as information can be adulterated over time. Meanings are changed and inevitably the original thought is sometimes lost. Many books have been written on this fact so we won't ventilate this here; however, oral traditions have their merit as many cultural traditions have lasted thousands of years, just through speaking what was learnt from the past.

However another danger looms. Though we have ample technological resources available to us today so we do not have to rely on oral traditions alone, we have more effective ways of preserving our history, we have copiers and computers with thousands of bytes of space for storing information that we can retrieve at the click of a button yet we seem to be less knowledgeable about the ways and acts of God today than before. Why is this so?

> "And they rejected his statutes, and his covenant that he made with their fathers, and his testimonies which he testified against them; and they followed vanity, and became vain, and went after the heathen that *were* round about them, *concerning* whom the LORD had charged them, that they should not do like them." 2 Kings 17:15

The writer of the book of Kings chronicles in this chapter the reason for Samaria's fall and exile. There was a rejecting of the statutes and covenant that their forefathers had made with God. This led them to follow after vanities, thus becoming vain themselves. Inevitably, this caused them to go after the heathen ways that were round about them. This was the same pattern as during the days of the Judges, it followed suit during the era of the Kings. When the ways of the Lord are rejected God's people will go after vanity. It was so <u>then</u>, it is so <u>now</u>. When you examine the reason for many of the failures of the Kings of Israel, it is stated that they did not follow the Lord, like their father David. In fact after the death of King David and King Solomon, the Kingdom was divided between north and south, Samaria and Judea. When a King did what was right in the sight of the Lord he was compared to King David.

"Twenty and five years old was he when he began to reign; and he reigned twenty and nine years in Jerusalem. His mother's name also *was* Abi, the daughter of Zachariah.

And he did *that which was* right in the sight of the LORD, according to all that David his father did." 2 Kings 18:2-3

This was King Hezekiah born hundreds of years after King David but he was still called his son why? He followed the ways of the Lord; he walked in the ways of the old covenant and didn't seek his own ways.

We don't have to go so far away from the reign of David. His grandson Rehoboam, Solomon's son is a perfect example. After being crowned king, the people of his Kingdom became agitated about their suffering, they asked,

"Thy father made our yoke grievous: now therefore make thou the grievous service of thy father, and his heavy yoke which he put upon us, lighter, and we will serve thee." 1 Kings 12:4

It was a reasonable request, after years of oppression from a King who rejected God. Solomon started very well, but at the end of his life he worshipped many idols and oppressed his own people, unlike his father David. It is recorded that Rehoboam consulted with the old men that stood before Solomon and they advised him to listen to the people, and speak good words to them, then they would be his servants forever.

"But he forsook the counsel of the old men, which they had given him, and consulted with the young men that were grown up with him, *and* which stood before him:"1Kings12:8

What was recorded next shows how a united Kingdom can easily be destroyed as Rehoboam followed the counsel of his peers which was opposite to the wisdom of the old advisors. King Rehoboam could only see his present situation, his actions, he was unsure of the eternal consequences of his words. 1 Kings 12:1-33 outlines the story:

"And Rehoboam went to Shechem: for all Israel were come to Shechem to make him king.

And it came to pass, when Jeroboam the son of Nebat, who was yet in Egypt, heard *of it,* (for he was fled from the presence of king Solomon, and Jeroboam dwelt in Egypt;)

That they sent and called him. And Jeroboam and all the congregation of Israel came, and spake unto Rehoboam, saying,

Thy father made our yoke grievous: now therefore make thou the grievous service of thy father, and his heavy yoke which he put upon us, lighter, and we will serve thee.

And he said unto them, Depart yet *for* three days, then come again to me. And the people departed.

And king Rehoboam consulted with the old men, that stood before Solomon his father while he yet lived, and said, How do ye advise that I may answer this people?

And they spake unto him, saying, If thou wilt be a servant unto this people this day, and wilt serve them, and answer them, and speak good words to them, then they will be thy servants for ever.

But he forsook the counsel of the old men, which they had given him, and consulted with the young men that were grown up with him, *and* which stood before him:

And he said unto them, What counsel give ye that we may answer this people, who have spoken to me, saying, Make the yoke which thy father did put upon us lighter?

And the young men that were grown up with him spake unto him, saying, Thus shalt thou speak unto this people that spake unto thee, saying, Thy father made our yoke heavy, but make thou *it* lighter unto us; thus shalt thou say unto them, My little *finger* shall be thicker than my father's loins.

And now whereas my father did lade you with a heavy yoke, I will add to your yoke: my father hath chastised you with whips, but I will chastise you with scorpions.

So Jeroboam and all the people came to Rehoboam the third day, as the king had appointed, saying, Come to me again the third day.

And the king answered the people roughly, and forsook the old men's counsel that they gave him;

And spake to them after the counsel of the young men, saying, My father made your yoke heavy, and I will add to your yoke: my father *also* chastised you with whips, but I will chastise you with scorpions.

Wherefore the king hearkened not unto the people; for the cause was from the LORD, that he might perform his saying, which the LORD spake by Ahijah the Shilonite unto Jeroboam the son of Nebat.

So when all Israel saw that the king hearkened not unto them, the people answered the king, saying, What portion have we in David? neither *have we* inheritance in the son of Jesse: to your tents, O Israel: now see to thine own house, David. So Israel departed unto their tents.

But *as for* the children of Israel which dwelt in the cities of Judah, Rehoboam reigned over them.

Then king Rehoboam sent Adoram, who *was* over the tribute; and all Israel stoned him with stones, that he died. Therefore king Rehoboam made speed to get him up to his chariot, to flee to Jerusalem.

So Israel rebelled against the house of David unto this day.

And it came to pass, when all Israel heard that Jeroboam was come again, that they sent and called him unto the congregation, and made him king over all Israel: there was none that followed the house of David, but the tribe of Judah only.

And when Rehoboam was come to Jerusalem, he assembled all the house of Judah, with the tribe of Benjamin, an hundred and fourscore thousand chosen men, which were warriors, to fight against the house of Israel, to bring the kingdom again to Rehoboam the son of Solomon.

But the word of God came unto Shemaiah the man of God, saying,

Speak unto Rehoboam, the son of Solomon, king of Judah, and unto all the house of Judah and Benjamin, and to the remnant of the people, saying,

Thus saith the LORD, Ye shall not go up, nor fight against your brethren the children of Israel: return every man to his house; for this thing is from me. They hearkened therefore to the word of the LORD, and returned to depart, according to the word of the LORD.

Then Jeroboam built Shechem in mount Ephraim, and dwelt therein; and went out from thence, and built Penuel.

And Jeroboam said in his heart, Now shall the kingdom return to the house of David:

If this people go up to do sacrifice in the house of the LORD at Jerusalem, then shall the heart of this people turn again unto their lord, *even* unto Rehoboam king of Judah, and they shall kill me, and go again to Rehoboam king of Judah.

Whereupon the king took counsel, and made two calves *of* gold, and said unto them, It is too much for you to go up to Jerusalem: behold thy gods, O Israel, which brought thee up out of the land of Egypt.

And he set the one in Bethel, and the other put he in Dan.

And this thing became a sin: for the people went *to worship* before the one, *even* unto Dan.

And he made an house of high places, and made priests of the lowest of the people, which were not of the sons of Levi.

And Jeroboam ordained a feast in the eighth month, on the fifteenth day of the month, like unto the feast that *is* in Judah, and he offered upon the altar. So did he in Bethel, sacrificing unto the calves that he had made: and he placed in Bethel the priests of the high places which he had made.

So he offered upon the altar which he had made in Bethel the fifteenth day of the eighth month, *even* in the month which he had devised of his own heart; and ordained a feast unto the children of Israel: and he offered upon the altar, and burnt incense.

Today

As many of the new leaders begin their reign they have stepped into a place of power and authority they did not fight to possess. Thus they have acquired privilege without sacrifice. They believe they were destined to lead, it is their calling. Their rise to power was fuelled not by a passion for the things of God but rather it has been fuelled by the applause of their peers. They have implemented godly principles which have brought them good success, now armed with success they have gone ahead to build their own kind of kingdom. They have built seeker sensitive movements, founded on the platforms of 'do not offend the people' because we need their money to take the gospel to the less fortunate. What wickedness! Who is more unfortunate than those who have taken the kingdom by a means other than humility? They are to be pitied, prayed for and delivered.

I declare to those who are serving God faithfully in what seems to be obscurity, where you are not appreciated for your gifts or grace. Just hold on to your God, those who flourish today will wither tomorrow like real grass. You do not have to chase the latest church growth model, seek first the kingdom of God and his righteousness, no matter how long it takes and he will add all things to you in due season.

The Christian giants of the past all had their weaknesses, from Biblical times all the way through to now. Let us not be so distracted by their failure that we miss their lessons. David learnt how to rule from his predecessor. He learnt that everything that King Saul did he should do the opposite. We must rediscover the value of our fathers. Fatherhood has been under attack from the garden until now; Satan has always gone after the man-child. The voice of Father brings instruction, discipline and power. So we have a generation growing up without instruction, they lack discipline and they wield a false power. The Lord is calling us back to the old beaten path, not for us to sit there and reminisce or to build altars, no; but so we can learn his ways and know his heart. In so doing we will move forward with a greater sense of purpose and confidence.

Many sons or young successful preachers are choosing for themselves fathers. This is an aberration. Fathers give birth to sons, not the other way around. If a pastor needs a spiritual father he should serve an older man until he is re-commissioned and sent. Many are using the term spiritual covering so flippantly today; it has lost all meaning and significance, as preachers pair up with preachers who they are comfortable with, or who can open doors for them. This is not fatherhood; this is commercial prostitution of the holy things of God. But "a seed shall serve him", amongst the filth and mire of today's Christianity there are godly ministries, godly fathers, godly sons, holy congregations. Yes, there are many, just not very visible, God is now clearing the stage of the false.

<u>Tomorrow</u>

You are called to be used of God today because tomorrow matters. The next generation must come to know the true and living God.

> "They shall come, and shall declare his righteousness unto a people that shall be born…"
> Psalm 22:31

There are those already born and there are those to be born who need to hear about Him, and only those truly used of God will declare the truth. This is where it starts; the Holy Spirit has empowered you for this purpose to declare Him.

Our days might seem gloomy now, but I believe that the days ahead will be as bright as the noon day sun, as a generation rises up who would not have rejected the words, ways and works of their fathers. But, rather they would have waited in the presence of God, until their time to be unleashed on their generation. The revelations of yesterday are what we stand on today to give further revelation, to light the way for those who are coming after us. We are not called by our names, we have no title, we are known as a voice, we are those who are being used of God.

A Simple Prayer

Lord, I simply desire to be used by you; I have come to realize that I have no other reason for existing. I tremble at your words as they take root in my life. And now Lord grant to your servant that with all boldness I may speak your word, in the name of Jesus Christ your only begotten son. Amen

ENDNOTES

i   Katz, Arthur, *Apostolic Foundations.* 2008, 257

ii   Katz, Arthur, *Apostolic Foundations.* 2008, Preface

iii   Katz Arthur, *Apostolic Foundations.* 2008, 85

iv   Murillo, Mario, *Fresh Fire.* Danville, CA: Anthony Douglas Publishing, 1991, 19

v   Strong, James, *Strong's Exhaustive Concordance of the Bible.* Peabody, MA, Hendrickson Publishers. Pg.115

vi   Wikipedia.org Fanny Crosby

vii   Wikipedia.org Fanny Crosby

viii   Katz, Arthur, Apostolic *Foundations. 2008,* 139

ix   Joyner, Rick, *There Were Two Trees in the Garden.* Charlotte NC, Morning Star Publication, 1992, 124